Connie and Vicki are sisters, friends, and colleagues. They have been in business together for many years. This is the first book they have written together.

Life would be easy if . . .
everyone had loving parents like ours.

Dedicated to our parents:
Bill and Kathy Purvis

Life Would Be Easy If It Weren't for OTHER People

Connie Podesta

with Vicki Sanderson

Illustrations by M. Loys Raymer

CORWIN PRESS, INC.
A Sage Publications Company
Thousand Oaks, California

For information:

Corwin Press, Inc.
A Sage Publications Company
2455 Teller Road
Thousand Oaks, California 91320
E-mail: order@corwinpress.com

SAGE Publications Ltd.
6 Bonhill Street
London EC2A 4PU
United Kingdom

SAGE Publications India Pvt. Ltd.
M-32 Market
Greater Kailash I
New Delhi 110 048 India

Printed in the United States of America

Library of Congress Cataloging-in-Publication Data

Podesta, Connie.
    Life would be easy if it weren't for other people / Connie Podesta, with Vicki Sanderson.
      p. cm.
    Includes index.
    ISBN 978-0-8039-6864-6
    ISBN 978-0-8039-6865-3
    1. Interpersonal conflict. 2. Interpersonal communication. 3. Interpersonal relations. I. Sanderson, Vicki. II. Title.
    BF637.I48 P63 1999
    158.2—dc21
                                                            99-6030

This book is printed on acid-free paper.

07 08 09 10 9 8

Production Editor: S. Marlene Head
Editorial Assistant: Kristen L. Gibson
Typesetter: Rebecca Evans
Cover Designer: Tracy E. Miller

CONTENTS

ABOUT THE AUTHORS

Connie Podesta is a licensed professional counselor, international professional speaker, keynoter, and trainer. She also is an actress, comedienne, songwriter, and playwright. She has addressed more than a million people throughout the world in all areas of business and industry, healthcare, and education. She has a B.S. in communications and speech and an M.S. in human relations. Her work as director of employee assistance and director of staff development in large organizations, as well as her experience as an educator, business owner, and consultant to some of the top Fortune 500 companies, has given her a unique insight into today's business world. Podesta also is the author of *How to Be the Person Successful Companies Fight to Keep* and *Self-Esteem and the Six-Second Secret*. She lives in Dallas with her husband and has two grown daughters.

Vicki Sanderson is a national professional speaker. She specializes in keynote addresses, customized workshops and seminars, inservice training, and after-dinner speaking. She has been an invited speaker for many corporations, associations, educational institutions, healthcare providers, and community organizations nationwide on a variety of topics. She has a B.A. in speech communications and radio/television. Her background as a speech communications teacher, business consultant, speaker, humorist, songwriter, author, and owner of her own company brings wisdom, experience, and knowledge to the writing of this book. She lives in Dallas with her husband, and they have one daughter.

INTRODUCTION

Do you have someone in your life who absolutely drives you out of your mind? In fact, if that person were to disappear off the face of the earth while you were reading this book, would your life greatly improve? If so, then this is the book for you. Let's face it: most of us work, commute, socialize, and even live with people who are not the easiest to be around. Most of the stress people experience, both personally and professionally, centers around other people and the often frustrating, confusing, and even contentious relationships we have with them.

As an educator, counselor, employee assistance director, and professional speaker, I have spent a good part of my life listening to and counseling men and women of all ages, and I have learned one important fact:

Most of the problems and stress people experience involve other people with whom communication is not easy.

Most people agree that "life would be easy if it weren't for *other* people." In fact, as a therapist, I seldom experienced anyone who came into my office and said, "Connie, I need help. I am a problem to everyone I come in contact with, and I would like to change some of my attitudes and behaviors." Instead, people began by telling me that they were okay, but that there was someone else in their life who was definitely *not okay*, and they needed my advice on how to deal with that difficult person.

1

Because the perception exists that it is "other people" with whom we live and work who create most of our turmoil and add insanity to an otherwise sane existence, it is important for us to understand and learn how to deal with and react to these people we would label as *difficult*.

To clarify an important point, this book is *not* about the one-time encounter with a difficult person in a rush-hour traffic jam, busy grocery store line, car servicing center, or other isolated confrontations with strangers. In those situations, use any short-term strategies available to extricate yourself as soon as possible with your dignity intact. Rather, Vicki and I will be discussing the person or persons with whom you have ongoing relationships: your friends, family, spouse, significant other, child, teenager, coworker, customer, boss, and so forth.

I HAVE READ ENOUGH BOOKS ON DIFFICULT PEOPLE!

You may be saying to yourself, "Difficult people? Is that what this book is all about? Isn't there enough written on that subject already?" It is true that there are many informative and interesting books on the subject of dealing, coping, and living with difficult people. These resources often offer the reader some fascinating techniques to use when faced with the friendly-challenged personality. But, the problem is that in order for even the most researched and successful strategies to work, the person using them must also have a thorough insight into what makes people (including ourselves) behave the way we do. Without this important understanding of human behavior, even the best techniques (tones of voice, body language, eye contact, etc.) usually fail to achieve the desired outcome, which is to improve communication and, in turn, establish a healthier, long-term relationship.

WILL THIS TAKE A LOT OF WORK? I'M PRETTY BUSY.

This book is definitely not a "quick fix." If that is what you are looking for, then this is not the book for you. In order for any significant change to take place in your life (such as finally getting along with a few difficult, frustrating individuals), taking the time to do it right is a necessary factor. Focusing on long-term solutions is far more beneficial than a short-term bandage.

In fact, quick fixes often cause the problem to become worse. For example, look at our society's focus (sometimes preoccupation) with weight. We have all heard that dieting is seldom effective by itself, yet thousands of people each year flock to every new weight-loss gimmick they learn about in the hopes that they can indeed "look fit in 21 days!" When I counseled men and women who were desperate to lose weight, the first obstacle was to convince them they must stop focusing on the word *diet* as a verb—something we do to ourselves. Instead, I helped them view *diet* as a noun—something that is incorporated into our daily life. This perception forces people interested in weight loss to concentrate first on changing some of their attitudes, ideas, and habits, which takes time. Habits do not change in 21 days.

The same philosophy is true when it comes to dealing with difficult people. There is no easy solution, wonder phrase, magical tone, gesture, or facial expression that can *alone* solve the problems most of us encounter when trying to communicate with people who do not act, behave, or react appropriately or effectively. Just as maintaining a healthy lifestyle is a long-term commitment based on a deeper understanding of ourselves, so is developing and maintaining healthy communication patterns and relationships. We must be willing to first look at ourselves and answer some tough, personal questions honestly.

- Why do I act and react the way I do?
- How do I choose to communicate in most situations?
- What attitudes and behaviors am I willing to change in myself that may, in turn, change the way other people treat and communicate with me?
- What role and part do I play in my most frustrating relationships, both personal and professional?

WAIT A MINUTE! I THOUGHT THIS BOOK WAS ABOUT OTHER PEOPLE, NOT ABOUT ME.

You may be thinking, "Are you saying it's my fault that these other people are treating me this way? Are you saying that there aren't people everywhere who are simply rude, insensitive, whiney, apathetic, and controlling? What about them?" You are right. There are plenty of "them" around, and they do indeed make our lives miserable. But, we must first understand what makes them tick, which does not mean you have to excuse them, love them, live with them, or even forgive them. In order to "deal" with them though, we must identify *why* they act the way they do and *why* we react the way we do. Then, will we be able to learn more about the part we play in that relationship. The reality is that some of the techniques we use that we believe will deter or even stop their behavior, may instead be what causes their behavior to continue or even become worse.

We must also be willing to admit one thing:

---

*Each of us can be and has been the
difficult person at times in our lives.*

It is as important for us to recognize our own difficult behaviors and strategies as it is to identify these in others. That is the unique difference and challenge in this book. The essential question is, "Are you as committed to learning about yourself as you are to learning about other people?" If so, this book could change your life.

YES, I WANT TO LEARN MORE ABOUT OTHER PEOPLE AND MYSELF. NOW WHAT?

Then get ready to begin a journey with me and Vicki, my sister and colleague—a journey that will lead you to the point where you can, perhaps for the first time, learn to successfully improve some of the troublesome relationships in your life? Settle back, relax, and read on, and you will discover some fascinating information about yourself and the people with whom you love, live, socialize, and work.

THE GOOD NEWS AND BAD NEWS

Let's begin with the question I hear repeatedly from men and women of all ages: "Why would anyone *choose* to be rude, obnoxious, sullen, apathetic, and so forth, rather than be friendly, optimistic, considerate, and supportive?" To answer that question, we must go back to our early childhood years when our basic personalities were beginning to take shape.

Difficult people have been trained and taught to act the way they do since they were children. In fact, they have been *rewarded* for their negative behavior throughout their entire lives. Difficult behavior worked for them as children and more important, it continues to work for them as adults.

I sincerely believe that most of us are born with the capacity and desire to love and be loved. As infants, we thrive on being spoken to, held, and touched. We respond enthusiastically to the simplest forms of affection—smiling, rocking, and cooing. As we grow, we learn to respond to verbal and visual cues, and we begin to adjust our behavior to obtain the positive responses we want. Throughout our lives, and especially during infancy, our actions are driven by our needs and our desire to meet those needs. As babies, we intuitively know to cry or scream in order to be fed, changed, or held. As we grow older, we begin to identify and match our behaviors with the responses they generate, and we consequently record those reactions in our subconscious. Each action causes our subconscious to ask, "Were my needs met as a result of what I just said or did?"

HOW DO WE STORE ALL THIS INFORMATION?

Imagine our subconscious as an internal filing cabinet where information is stored under either "Positive—that behavior worked. Try it again," or "Negative—that behavior didn't work. Try something else next time." As our behaviors slowly sort themselves into these two files, our future adult personalities begin to take shape. You will often hear these initial learning periods referred to as *phases*, and we continue to move through these phases throughout our childhood and adolescence. Basically, childhood phases (or stages) are simply those early formative times in everyone's life when we all explored every form of behavior until we figured out which ones caused our parents, caregivers, and teachers to give us what we needed. How these early role models responded to us during these crucial learning periods will have a lasting impact on our emerging adult personality.

The game of life is mostly about "getting our needs met." Once our very basic human needs of food and shelter are taken care of, most of what we say and do revolves around our need to be loved, liked, recognized, appreciated, and respected by other people whom we view as necessary or important. How we play this game of life depends on how we learned to communicate and behave while growing up. In other words, what did we have to do to get our needs met? As children, some of us got our needs met as a result of our positive behavior. We asked respectfully, smiled nicely or said, "please." On the other hand, some of our needs were met as a result of negative behavior when we whined, cried, or threw a tantrum. When a certain behavior produces a positive result (candy, money, attention, etc.), we file this information in the drawer that says, "Works great! Do it again." Therefore, children whose needs were met when they acted respectfully, lovingly, and responsibly tend to continue to use positive behaviors as adults, and the children whose needs were met as a result of being nasty, hurtful, pouty, sarcastic, or mean will continue to use more negative behaviors throughout their life.

It is important to understand that a child who can successfully and repeatedly manipulate adults will quickly learn to enjoy the ensuing feelings of power and control that occur as a result of that manipulation. In time, the need to be loved, liked, and appreciated may be secondary to the need to be in charge and in control. The need to be respected may be sacrificed for or confused with the need to feel

power over others. This is why difficult people often make us feel powerless and seem to enjoy the control they have over us. They are still using the same childhood manipulative tricks many years later.

HOW DO I PLAY A PART IN ALL OF THIS?

If someone is consistently behaving toward you in ways that are inappropriate or unacceptable, then the first and most important step is to ask yourself, "Am I in any way rewarding their negative behavior?" This is the toughest question for most of us to answer. Naturally, we rarely view our responses and reactions to unacceptable, inappropriate, or even abusive behavior as positive or rewarding. But, let's look at some examples where a reaction that was intended to be a deterrent was, instead, viewed as a reward by the other person.

Situation 1. Harry wants to play golf on Saturday, but every time he mentions it to Helen, she gets upset and begins to argue.

Rather than face a 2-hour lecture, he usually finds it easier to just stay home. One day, however, Harry gets angry and starts to yell at Helen accusing her of being a nag and never understanding him. Instead of answering back, Helen gets her feelings hurt and stomps off, giving him the silent treatment. Because she is not talking anyway, Harry decides to take advantage of her "cold shoulder" and go play a few holes of golf. In this instance, Harry behaved badly by yelling and using inappropriate threats. He was consequently ignored, which in this case is definitely a reward as far as Harry is concerned, because it left him free to get his needs met. He played golf the rest of the day!

Lesson learned: Do not ask nicely to play golf because you will not get permission. Instead, yell and scream and you will be left alone to do whatever you want.

Situation 2. Jennifer is in the second grade and does not like recess. She is new to the school and none of the children talk to her. Some of the other children even make fun of her. When she asks the teacher if she can stay in, the teacher says, "Oh no, Jennifer. Everyone has to go outside and play. You'll have fun." One day, Jennifer has a fight with another little girl and pushes her down. The teacher tells Jennifer that fighting is against the rules, and she will have to stay inside for recess.

Lesson learned: Ask the teacher respectfully to stay indoors and you will not get what you want. Push someone and you can avoid recess.

Situation 3. Jeremy, a teenager, loves to go up to his room immediately following dinner. But Mom, who is recently divorced, gets lonely and likes to have his company while watching television. Every time Jeremy tries to tell his mom that he wants to go upstairs she gets her feelings hurt, so he feels guilty and stays with her. One night, however, he's expecting a phone call from his girlfriend. When his mom gives him a hard time, he begins to yell and says, "I hate you!" His mom, trying to teach Jeremy that yelling is not acceptable behavior, sends him to his room.

Lesson learned: If you want to spend the evening alone, away from your mom, just yell and be disrespectful. Then you will be sent to your room for an evening of peace and quiet.

Situation 4. Staff has been cut back at Company X and everyone is working harder than ever. Jason needs help with a special customer and asks John, who is nearby doing nothing, for help. John becomes angry and says, "That's not my job," in front of the customer. Jason does not want to make a scene, so he asks another employee and before long, the word is out and no one ever approaches John for help.

Lesson learned: All you have to do to get away with the least amount of work is to refuse to cooperate and cause a public scene. You will continue to get paid and everyone will leave you alone.

These are just a few examples of how difficult behavior is rewarded. Please take note: ignoring or avoiding the difficult person or their behavior is usually viewed by the subconscious as a *positive* response.

Each time we respond to another person, we have three choices. We can:

1. Be positive
2. Be negative
3. Choose to avoid or ignore them.

As discussed previously, a positive response will be filed in the drawer that says, "It worked. Do it again." A negative response is usually filed in the drawer that says, "Not so good. Try something else." Ironically, the avoidance or ignore response is often viewed by the subconscious of the receiver in the same way they would view a positive response. In other words, that behavior also will be filed by the receiver in the drawer that says, "Great! Do it again."

WHY IS AVOIDANCE SEEN AS POSITIVE?

There are only two reasons for you to ever ignore someone's unacceptable behavior:

1. You did not notice their behavior and, therefore, were not aware of the behavior.
2. You noticed the behavior, but you do not mind if it occurs again.

Consistently ignoring and avoiding difficult people is
one of the biggest mistakes we can make if we seriously
want our relationship with them to improve.

Yet, ignoring them is often the response and reaction that many people give because it is easier than confronting the issue. This does not mean that there are not times when avoiding a confrontation is the best choice, but it does mean that consistently ignoring poor behavior is, in and of itself, a reward for that behavior. In fact, many difficult people love to be ignored or avoided—it makes it all that much easier for them to get what they want with us out of their way!

IT IS HARD TO BELIEVE THAT WE REWARD DIFFICULT PEOPLE

Look at the average workplace today. Vicki and I work with companies throughout North America in all industries: education, healthcare, government, and business. Some are large Fortune 500 organizations and others are small, family-owned businesses. No matter what the business or where it is located (rural or urban), we continually witness the same scene: difficult people constantly getting what they want. Just take a look at your own home, office, church, committee, or association. Most difficult people get better schedules (we do not want to make them mad if they do not get the days off they want). Most difficult people get the easier customers (we simply *can't* give them our toughest customers). Difficult people are assigned fewer projects and asked to be on fewer committees. And, if that is not reward enough, they collect the same paycheck as every other worker who is trying to work hard, be cooperative, and do the right thing. We continually reward negative behavior by ignoring and avoiding their unacceptable behavior and then handing them a paycheck for a "job well done."

SO, WHAT DO WE DO WITH THESE DIFFICULT PEOPLE?

If you are like most people, you would like the difficult people in your life to change, grow up, face facts, get real, quit complaining, act their age, deal with it, work it out, get their act together, and stop playing games. We want them to transform and become rational, caring, decent human beings. Well, do not hold your breath because that is unlikely to happen as long as we continue to act and react to them the way we always have. In fact, does it not seem to you as though you have already tried everything to get them to change? You have probably yelled at them, cried, threatened, or perhaps have given them the silent treatment (something they never seem to mind at all). Perhaps you have tried to discuss the situation with them rationally or have spent hours pleading with them to change. You may have even left self-help books around, hoping they will read them. Maybe you have done nothing but play the martyr, and you think that if they really cared about you, they would simply know how you feel and try to change on their own, or perhaps you have complained about them to everyone who would listen and even dreamed (had nightmares!) about them while you were sleeping.

Let's be honest. How many of you have even resorted to a few difficult behaviors of your own, rationalizing that they deserve a taste of what they dish out? Even if they do not ruin our lives, they certainly have a way of consuming a great deal of our time and energy. So let's get inside the difficult person's head and see what makes them tick.

WHAT DO DIFFICULT PEOPLE REALLY WANT?

Difficult people want to do their own thing, in their own time, in their own way, and without any interference from us.

In addition, they expect everyone and everything around them to cooperate, even work extra hard if necessary, to ensure that this happens, and they do not see anything unreasonable about these expectations. Keep in mind that if someone has had a lifetime of behaving badly and getting rewarded, there has been little in their experience to signal them or teach them that their actions are unacceptable or inappropriate. In fact, they are easily irritated and disappointed because they expect the world to center around their needs and are let down when things do not go their way.

When difficult people do not get what they want, they usually complain, connive, yell, or mope—and do it so blatantly that the rest of us have no choice but to notice their "problems." Difficult people honestly believe that if they are miserable (as they almost always are), they have the right to make everyone within hearing distance miserable as well. They also have little, if any, desire or motivation

to alter their personalities or behaviors. If you doubt that, try asking them to make some minor personality adjustment. They won't take a deep breath before they defend themselves and proclaim that the qualities you find objectionable are just part of their personality. We have all heard them say defiantly, "This is just the way I am. I can't help it," or "I've always been this way," or "No one else has a problem with me but you." No matter how they phrase it, the implication is always the same. They are not changing and if we do not like it, too bad! We are just going to have to accept them the way they are. Difficult people often take it even one step further and imply that *we* are the ones who have a problem. Why would they believe that? Because so many people have been accepting and rewarding them for acting inappropriately for a long, long time.

We learn a lot from difficult people. We learn to tolerate their unacceptable behaviors and attitudes as "part of life." We learn to hold back our own feelings and swallow our words. We learn to make concessions, even when we do not receive anything in return and we compromise, even when it is 90/10 instead of 50/50. We learn to shrug our shoulders in a gesture of resignation when they start to unload their tales of woe (many difficult people act like the world's greatest victims) or we eat lunch in our offices by ourselves in order to have a moment's peace and quiet. We learn to go to the movies and restaurants *they* want to go to, without arguing or even hinting we would like to go somewhere else, having learned early on the futility of expressing our own opinions. We learn to clean up after them. We offer to work the weekend shift when it is their turn, telling ourselves that it is easier than listening to them complain that the schedule is unfair.

Many of us learn even more. We learn to lie for them. We learn to cover up and make excuses for them and, sadly, sometimes we even learn to accept abuse from them (verbal, physical, sexual, emotional). We learn to rescue them repeatedly until it seems the natural thing to do. When we have finally reached our wit's end, we still may be reluctant to confront the direct cause of our misery—the difficult person! Instead, we may become irritated with everyone else around us who is trying to help, especially if they are giving us advice (often very good advice) on how we should change the way *we* act and react. We may soon begin experiencing unhealthy levels of stress.

We may even question our own ability to relate and communicate with others. "Maybe it's me," we reason. Or, finally convinced that we must be responsible, we ask, "What am I doing to deserve this?" When the people I counsel get to this point, they usually want two things: sympathy and validation. These frustrated individuals want me to feel sorry that they are being treated this way, agree with them that it is *not* their fault and tell them that they are genuinely nice people who truly deserve to be treated better. Unfortunately, I cannot tell them these things because the truth is that we each play a very important role in our relationships with difficult people. In fact, without us playing our part, they might not even be as difficult. We also contribute and lay the groundwork for the unacceptable behavior being aimed in our direction. The reality is:

---

*Difficult people need our cooperation and our
permission to intimidate, control, and repeatedly
manipulate us in order to get their way.*

I HATE THE WAY THEY ACT. HOW DO I GIVE PERMISSION? THEIR BEHAVIOR IS NOT MY FAULT. I AM A VERY NICE PERSON.

The great irony is that it is often our very niceness and desire to get along at any cost that allows many difficult people to live up to their reputation. In a way, we draw them to us like iron to a magnet. Sadly, there is really a great deal of truth in the saying, "Nice guys finish last." Nice people are often the last to leave work, the last in the kitchen cleaning up, or the last to receive the promotion. Nice people are definitely the last to get their own needs met and are usually concerned that everyone else's needs be met first. By always being nice and giving in, we do our own part to encourage these gurus of contemptible behavior, these whiners, shouters, complainers, victims of the life-isn't-fair school of thought, and these perpetrators of doom and gloom.

How do we encourage difficult people? We encourage them by ignoring, avoiding, making excuses for, or simply giving in to their difficult behavior. How do we give permission? We allow their behavior by letting their actions go unchecked and by not making them accountable for how they behave. How do we cooperate? We cooperate by being so nice that we will give in and avoid an unpleasant scene rather than confront them when we disagree.

ARE YOU SAYING THAT I SHOULD NOT BE NICE? BUT, LOOK AT THE WORLD WITH ALL THE CRIME, VIOLENCE, AND ABUSE. DON'T YOU THINK WE COULD USE A FEW MORE "NICE" PEOPLE?

You are right. We do need more nice, caring, and decent people, as long as it is the confident, healthy, and functional kind of nice. Later in this book, we will go into more detail about the two kinds of nice: (a) passive-nice, or nice at any cost—keeping the peace and avoiding all hassles and confrontations even if it means giving in and going along no matter what, and (b) assertive-nice, which is caring and respecting yourself and others while working to improve healthy communication patterns and striving for a win/win environment. In order to be assertive-nice, a person must believe that each person has an obligation to treat others with respect, coupled with the equally important right to be treated with dignity and respect in return.

We are not saying that anyone deserves the kind of treatment difficult people are famous for, but the bottom line is:

In most relationships, we are treated exactly the way we allow ourselves to be treated.

Good news and bad news accompanies this reality. I have already told you the bad news: We are often responsible for giving permission to, and even rewarding the difficult people in our lives, thus playing an important part in the unhealthy development of these relationships. But, here is the good news: Because we are partly responsible, there is something we can do to stop the manipulative patterns and instead create and maintain relationships where we are being treated respectfully. In fact, that is not just good news, that is great news. We can do something much more effective than simply integrating short-term techniques and waiting for the difficult person to change. We can begin by focusing on ourselves and the changes we can make in our own behaviors and reactions. In other words, we can begin immediately to take control of how other people treat us.

CAN WE EVER CHANGE THE DIFFICULT PERSON?

No, no, and no again! Unfortunately, people are trying to change other people constantly even though they have been told over and over again that it will never work. We try to change our children, friends, spouses, significant others, coworkers, and even our parents (as though after 60, 70, even 80 years they will finally listen to us)! The reality is that as long as we are trying to change them, we will never be in control of our own reactions, emotions, and well-being. When we are trying to change other people, we invariably begin to act inappropriately ourselves. We may even become as difficult as they are and begin resorting to our own manipulations. Perhaps we begin to whine or cry, maybe complain or gripe, or yell and scream. Whenever any of us begins to behave in an unacceptable or manipulative way, it is the signal that we are feeling out of control at that moment, and in order to regain control we unconsciously revert to the irrational, win/lose techniques that worked so well for us as children.

WHAT HAVE WE LEARNED SO FAR?

If we become like them, they will not change. If we give in because they manipulated us and behaved inappropriately, they will not change. If we ignore their actions, they will not change. And, if we reward their behavior by helping them get their needs met, they will not change. In fact, these reactions will only ensure that their annoying, whining, intimidating, controlling behavior will continue and become more frequent and exaggerated as time goes by. However, when we accept responsibility for our own actions and reactions, we *can* regain control of our lives and, in turn, our self-esteem and well-being.

So, the really good news is that there is much we can change if we are willing to take a deep and honest look at ourselves and learn exactly *why* we do what we do and act the way we act. Are you ready to take charge of your life? If so, difficult people: get ready to step aside!

Summary

- Difficult people have been trained and taught to act the way they do since they were children.
- Difficult people want to do their own thing, in their own time, in their own way, without interference.
- Children who can manipulate their parents soon learn to enjoy feelings of power and control over others.
- We reward difficult people by giving in to their needs.
- We cannot change difficult people, we can only change ourselves and our reactions to their behavior.

- When we ignore unacceptable, inappropriate behavior, it will usually happen again because our avoidance tells the difficult person that we are willing to accept their behavior.
- In most relationships, we are treated exactly the way we allow ourselves to be treated.

Take Action

- Think about two difficult people in your life.
- Identify the behaviors of these difficult people.
- Ask yourself if you could possibly be rewarding these difficult people.
- Would they describe you as the difficult person? If so, what would they say?

2

THE BASICS

There are four basic communication/behavior patterns:

Assertive
Aggressive
Passive
Passive-Aggressive

Every time we speak, we communicate by using one of these four styles. We will go into greater detail on each of these four behavior patterns in later chapters, but right now we just want to introduce them to you. It is important to note that

---

Only *assertive* communication models
healthy, productive communication.

The other three styles are full of tricks, devious behaviors, and manipulative gimmicks. Unfortunately, they usually comprise the vast majority of people's communication with each other. I am sure that you will be able to quickly identify many people in your life who use each of these four styles, and, if you are really honest, you will see that you have used each of these styles at different times in your life as well. The reality of human interaction is that we all move in and out of these patterns continuously throughout our life. However, it is important to remember:

We always have a choice of which communication
style we will use in every given situation.

The style we choose generally depends on what our past experiences have taught us will work best to get our needs met in each specific situation. Understanding these four communication styles will help you learn how to react most effectively when confronted with a difficult person. It will also help you to recognize when you are using manipulative behavior to get your own needs met. (Oh, I know, it is difficult to admit that you can be perceived as difficult by others, but remember, your friends and family may be reading this book right now to learn how to deal with you!)

WAIT A MINUTE . . . SOMETIMES
I'M THE DIFFICULT PERSON?

We all know difficult people and, we can all be the difficult person. The goal of this book is to reduce this behavior in others and ourselves. Changing ourselves through honest reflection is not always an easy task, but just think of the benefits. Learning to understand ourselves better will allow us to have closer and more supportive relationships, well-deserved peace of mind, better health, and more energy to spend on our family and career! Now that is worth it, right?

Let's begin with the most effective and healthiest communication style, which is called *assertive*. We use the assertive style only at the times when our self-esteem is intact, giving us the confidence to communicate without games and manipulation. When we are being assertive, we work hard to create mutually satisfying solutions to problems that may occur. We communicate our needs clearly and forthrightly. We care about the relationship and strive for a win/win situation; however, we know our own limits and refuse to be pushed beyond them just because someone else wants or needs something from us. Most of us would agree that this is how we would like to communicate with others and have them communicate with us. Yet, assertive is the style most people use least. We will learn why in chapter 3.

The next communication style is *aggressive*, which *always* involves manipulation. The two emotions used most often to manipulate others are hurt and anger. We may attempt to make people do what we want by inducing guilt (hurt) or by using intimidation and control tactics (anger). Aggressive communication employs techniques such as whining, yelling, pouting, screaming, complaining, crying, or getting one's feelings hurt. Whichever behavior we choose (hurt or anger), the goal is the same: We get our needs met through the manipulation of others. Whether it is covert manipulation by feigning hurt or overt intimidation by expressing hostility or anger, it is still aggressive because there is no concern for creating a win/win outcome. We simply want our needs met, *now*!

WHAT IS THE DIFFERENCE BETWEEN ASSERTIVE AND AGGRESSIVE?

Many people often confuse the assertive and aggressive communication styles, but the truth is that they are completely opposite of one another. Aggressive behavior involves force, manipulation, or mental or physical coercion to get others to do what is wanted. Assertive behavior *never* involves force, manipulation, or coercion. There should be no confusing these two styles of communication.

In a relationship, assertiveness exhibits great self-confidence, whereas aggressiveness exhibits a lack of self-confidence. Although there are a few arenas where aggressive behavior is called for (such as participating in sports or war), aggressiveness is *never* going to work in a relationship. Sadly, even war might be avoided if the parties concerned could learn to be more assertive and strive to mediate and negotiate rather than use violence and force to solve their problems. Even aggressive sports, such as football, rely heavily on team members and coaches to rationally think of strategies that could win the game.

IF WE DECIDE TO "GIVE IN," WHAT STYLE IS THAT?

A third communication style is called *passive*. Most everyone has experienced this state of compliance—the "I'll do whatever you want, it's better than a fight" attitude at some time in their life. When we are being passive, we do not talk much, question even less, and actually do very little—we simply try not to rock the boat. Ever heard the phrase, "go along to get along?" That phrase describes the passive personality style. People who use passive techniques avoid hassles at all costs. When we are in our passive mode, we do not complain or confront—or contribute, for that matter. Passives have learned that it is safer not to react and better to disappear than to stand up and become noticed.

WHY IS THE FOURTH STYLE CALLED PASSIVE-AGGRESSIVE?

The fourth style combines a little aggressive behavior and a little passive behavior, and so it is labeled *passive-aggressive*. When we are in the passive-aggressive mode, our goal may be to pay someone back, get even, teach someone a lesson, or make someone wish they had never been born. You probably remember being there, both as the perpetrator and the victim. Honestly, isn't there someone in your life right this minute who needs to be "taught a thing or two?" Have you already formulated the plan for getting even? Are you looking forward to making them suffer . . . just a teeny bit? If so, you are about to step into the world of the passive-aggressive. Devious and sneaky, passive-aggressives try to get their way without confronting others or asserting themselves. The passive-aggressive style avoids direct confrontation (passive), but manipulates to get even (aggressive).

DO EACH OF US, AT TIMES, USE ALL FOUR OF THE COMMUNICATION PATTERNS?

As we stated earlier, most of us use each of the four communication styles at different times with different people in different situations. We can be assertive with a client, passive with our manager, aggressive with our children, and passive-aggressive with a friend— all in one day! It is quite remarkable how quickly full-grown adults can exhibit the behaviors of children when they feel thwarted. Even the most well-adjusted individual among us is capable of resorting to childish tricks and manipulations when we feel our needs are not being met. However, regardless of the behavior style we use, it is still always our *choice* whether to communicate maturely and directly or to use one of the other three nonproductive styles.

In the next few chapters, we will discuss each style in depth, both in others and in ourselves. We will also give you tips and examples so you can replace the ineffective techniques found in the aggressive, passive, and passive-aggressive patterns of communication with some great new assertive options that can diffuse anger, reduce guilt, and build relationships. Our goal is to put you back in control of your life, both personally and professionally. If you are ready for that, then let's get started!

Summary

- There are four basic communication styles: assertive, aggressive, passive, and passive-aggressive.
- We can always choose which communication style to use.
- The only healthy communication style is assertive communication.
- *Aggressive* involves the use of hurt to invoke guilt or anger to invoke fear.
- Passive means to avoid confrontation at all costs.
- Passive-Aggressive involves paybacks and attempts to get even.
- Most of us use a combination of these four styles, depending on the person or situation.

Take Action

- Begin to pay attention to which communication styles you use throughout the day. How often do you use a communication style other than assertive?
- Watch and identify the communication styles some of the difficult people in your life use. Can you begin to notice how others use manipulative techniques to get their way?

3

THE ASSERTIVE PERSONALITY
Open, Honest, and Direct

Let's start by repeating one important fact for emphasis:

Assertive is the only one of the four communication styles that is considered a healthy and productive way to communicate.

For our purposes, *healthy communication* is defined as the ability to let others know our needs, concerns, and feelings in an open and honest way without game playing, gimmicks, threats, manipulations, or hidden agendas. When we choose to communicate assertively, we also set and enforce fair, consistent limits and boundaries, and can firmly say "no" if we are unable or unwilling to do what is asked of us. Being assertive requires a sincere belief on the part of the communicator that all individuals, including oneself, are valuable people who are worthy of being treated respectfully. The assertive style uses negotiation rather than manipulation, openness rather than secrecy, and honesty rather than game playing. When we are being assertive, we do not negate other people's feelings, denigrate their positions or belittle them personally. Instead, we rely on our interpersonal skills to see that our needs are met without resorting to negative tactics. When we are being assertive, we persuade and convince, rather than coerce and manipulate.

IS THE ASSERTIVE STYLE EFFECTIVE IN DEALING WITH DIFFICULT PEOPLE?

Assertive is the *only* communication style that is effective when dealing with difficult people. You might say that assertiveness is the "communication highway" to developing and maintaining good relationships, both personally and professionally. Imagine driving in your car and taking the quickest and safest route to a destination 200 miles away. It is a great trip and in just a short time, you arrive feeling at ease, relaxed, and ready to "do the town." That is assertive: having a goal in mind and communicating in the style that will help you reach that goal most effectively. Now, picture traveling in your car to the same destination, only this time you have a passenger. This is not just any passenger, but one who constantly requests you to detour, stop to go to the restroom, get a snack, or buy a souvenir. This passenger is very demanding. It takes all the energy and patience you have to reach your destination. When you finally do, you are too tired to enjoy yourself.

Difficult people are exactly like that passenger. They constantly strive to detour us from the path of clear and honest communication. Unfortunately, we usually allow them to set our course. No wonder we lose our way and become frustrated and confused! Assertiveness allows us to steer ourselves back on the right road. Assertiveness is the compass that keeps us going in the right direction while maintaining our professionalism, integrity, and sanity.

When we are being assertive, we understand that we have choices in our lives, and we know that we must always accept responsibility for our own actions. We use assertive communication to neutralize the efforts of others to manipulate us. We refuse to accept the premise promoted by the manipulator that the choices they offer are the only choices available. For instance, whiners hope that we do not see that there are other alternatives that will stop their whining, other than capitulation. Whiners want us to believe that their complaints will be stifled only by giving in to their demands. Likewise, people who show their tempers want us to believe that their anger will be so unpleasant that we would be much better off if we give in to their wishes.

Difficult people try to coerce us into meeting their demands by fostering the impression that our options are severely limited or nonexistent. Either we do things their way or we will suffer dire

consequences. When we are being assertive, however, we insist on entertaining all the options available, not just those offered by the difficult person. In the world of the assertive, each person is responsible for his or her own behavior. Assertive communication is open, honest, and does not react to coercion, force, whining, guilt, or put-downs.

> When we are assertive we choose to handle ourselves,
> our reactions, our relationships, and stressful situations in
> a healthy, responsible, and nonmanipulative manner.

Assertive may be the answer to many of our problems. However, in my experience, I discovered that most people spend far less time communicating assertively than they do communicating in the other three styles: aggressive, passive, and passive-aggressive. During counseling, most of my clients were quick to admit that their main reason for coming into therapy was because they were frustrated, saddened, or depressed because they could not talk to or communicate with some of the most important people in their lives: their spouse, child, parent, coworker, boss, neighbor, friend, and so forth. Not only were they tired of how they were being treated, they were also disappointed in their own behavior and reactions to that treatment. In other words, they realized that their responses to difficult people were neither productive nor satisfying. They were desperately seeking a way to communicate that would help both them and the difficult person learn to get along. Assertiveness is that answer.

IF ASSERTIVENESS IS THE BEST COMMUNICATION STYLE, WHY DO MOST PEOPLE USE IT THE LEAST?

As they were growing up, many people did not have role models who behaved assertively and showed them how to resolve conflict in an assertive, healthy way. Assertive people ask questions, seek answers, look at all points of view, and engage in meaningful, open-ended dialogue without anger, hurt feelings, or defensiveness. Does that sound like what goes on in the average home, school, or office? Often when children ask, "Why?," they are given the pat parental response, "Because I'm your parent and I said so and that's final!" Children are often encouraged to be passive at home. Many parents issue orders such as, "Do what I say and don't ask any questions," instead of modeling assertive techniques involving conflict resolution, negotiation, and meaningful discussion.

Although there are certainly many times when a child needs to follow instructions immediately for his own safety and well-being, there are also many missed opportunities for a child to learn to respectfully participate in discussions that will affect his or her life.

The key word here is *participate*. It does not mean that the parent should give up control. It does not even mean that consensus is necessary. A functional home must have someone in charge who is emotionally capable of making fair, healthy decisions. But, a home that models assertive communication is committed to helping children understand the reasons behind the choices that are being made and the rules being set. This helps the child learn to process information later as an adult so he can deal with difficult situations in an assertive manner.

Learning to express needs and concerns, solving problems, and participating in decision making will help children feel comfortable communicating openly and assertively as they grow up. When children are not allowed or encouraged to communicate their wants, fears, and concerns, they will soon begin to get their needs met by other means—usually through manipulation. At this point, the child will resort to communication using the other three styles: passive, aggressive, and passive-aggressive.

It has been my experience that when a parent responds, "Because I said so," to a child's inquiry of "Why?," it is often because the parent does not have a good reason. As parents, we might consider that if we cannot explain why we are doing something, perhaps it is because we are doing something that is unfair, unnecessary, or not well thought out. This does not mean children should be encouraged to argue every point, but it is usually helpful if they understand the reason for the decision so they can put it in some context they can draw from later in life.

Sometimes parents even tell children that what they are feeling is not accurate. Perhaps you have heard one of the following interactions:

"Mom, I'm tired."

—"No, you're not. You just got up from your nap."

"Dad, I'm hungry."

—"You can't be, you just ate lunch."

"Mom, I don't want to go to the party."

—"Sure you do, you'll have fun."

Unfortunately, these kinds of responses do not build the confidence in children that is needed—the confidence to trust and believe

in their own feelings. It is important to encourage our children to express their feelings of fear, distrust, and many other emotions as long as they are taught to do so in an appropriate and respectful way. It may make a parent's life more tedious at times, but it is vital for the child's development, especially in the world we live in today where, sadly, children cannot trust everyone they meet or everything they hear. When children are taught to distrust their feelings, they also learn to disregard crucial internal warning signs. For example, when a stranger approaches them, we want them to trust the signal that flashes, "Danger!" Asking questions and not accepting everything at face value can be important skills in today's world where every person a child encounters may not always be honest and good.

IF ASSERTIVENESS IS NOT ALWAYS MODELED AT HOME, THEN WHAT ABOUT AT SCHOOL? DO EDUCATORS ENCOURAGE STUDENTS TO EXPRESS THEIR FEELINGS AND ASK ASSERTIVE QUESTIONS?

I have been involved with schools and education for many years. I have been privileged to observe and work with educators who are committed to modeling compassionate, fair, cooperative, and honest behavior, thus opening the door for students to learn assertive communication skills that will follow them through life. These educators are to be commended for realizing that education is not just about textbooks and what a student learns. Education is also about *how* a student learns to integrate that information into their life, so they can be a better, more productive parent, spouse, employee, and community member. Unfortunately, not all teachers model such mature and professional behavior. In fact, some educators even discourage children from asking questions, relying instead on old-fashioned techniques such as lecture, memorization, and repeat-back-what-I-said testing. Often, foreign exchange students in the United States are confused by the lecture/memorization methods used by American educators because many European schools use the Socratic method, which is based on the assumption that the best learning takes place when students are engaged in critical thinking. Under this method, children are encouraged to debate with their teachers and question information rather than blindly accept material presented as fact. Students using this method are also encouraged to express doubt as to the validity of what is being taught, as long as they have the research to back up their comments. In other words, these students' grades are dependent on their willingness and resourcefulness to debate, argue, and question their teachers in a respectful way. In the United States, I have often observed some of the same curious youngsters get into trouble because their questioning and debating with the instructor has been taken personally, almost as though the teacher's integrity and authority had been attacked.

Assertive students are sometimes accused of talking back or being impertinent, not because their tone or body language indicates disrespect, but simply because they ask questions or express concerns or doubts about a parent or teacher's rule, advice, or information. Vicki and I speak to thousands of educators each year and we always talk about this very issue. We remind educators that it is imperative in today's global, competitive work environment that students be prepared to think and reason critically, question and debate the pros and cons in order to understand both points of view, and form fact-based opinions based on extensive research rather than blindly believe any information that they are exposed to at face-value. We are both excited and pleased at the large numbers of assertive, professional educators who respond that they already include these life skills as part of their basic curriculum.

ARE THERE OTHER AREAS IN OUR LIVES WHERE WE CONSISTENTLY WITNESS A LACK OF ASSERTIVE COMMUNICATION?

Yes. We see examples of nonassertive communication in all areas of our lives. For one, the media is not always a good model of assertiveness, as it increasingly resorts to sensationalism, appealing to our emotions instead of promoting reason. Television talk shows constantly feature relationships and families communicating every way but assertively. We witness first hand in the news every night the sad, nonproductive, even violent result of nonassertive relationships.

The following is another example: Think about the most recent political campaigns. Did you witness candidates asserting their positions and questioning their opponents on issues while discussing their own strengths and plans for the future? Most likely, the candidates simply tried to discredit one another. Political debate has often regressed to accusations of blame and shame, with the voter left to sort fact from fiction. One of the problems with a lack of assertiveness modeling and training is that assertive communication is absolutely necessary in order to effectively mediate, negotiate, and resolve conflicts—necessary skills for successful relationships, both personal and professional. If our country's political and media leaders fail to model healthy, assertive behavior and communication, then it becomes even more important for these skills to be taught at home and in school.

HOW IS OUR ABILITY TO SOLVE PROBLEMS AFFECTED BY A LACK OF ASSERTIVENESS?

We are often given models of problem solving that are not effective. Let's look at how most of us were taught to resolve conflict as we were growing up. First, think back to your childhood. You and a sibling or friend argued over a toy. Did someone teach you the skills you might use to negotiate the use of the toy? More likely, you were sent to separate rooms without the toy and only allowed to come out when you had "learned to get along." Just how were you supposed to learn to get along in a room by yourself?

That childhood example represents exactly how most conflict is handled throughout our lives. We take away the controversial object, policy, or person, separate the opposing sides, then later bring them back together and have them try it again, even though they usually received no training in the interim to prepare them any better for a second confrontation. No doubt, you can think of many situations in everyday life where conflict is not resolved in an assertive manner. Following are a few more examples:

Problem: Two children on a baseball team argue over whose turn it is to bat.

Typical solution: Remove the bat, put the kids on different teams or in a different lineup, and continue the game.

Problem: Two students talk during class.

Typical solution: Bring one to the front, leave one in the back, and continue class.

Problem: Two employees cannot work together.

Typical solution: Reschedule or reassign them so they are on different shifts, floors, committees, or departments, and avoid having them work together.

Do you see any assertive models of problem solving in those examples? In fact, the message is quite the opposite: do not confront, mediate, or learn to communicate together—instead, separate and avoid the problem! Is it any wonder the divorce rate is so high? At the first sign of real conflict, what comes to mind first is *separate*.

Separate at the first sign of conflict has been our model. I was always amazed at how many couples came into my office and told me, "We just can't talk to each other anymore. Do you think maybe we should separate for awhile?" My answer was always, "No! If you can't talk while living in the same house, what makes you think you'll learn to communicate on a more intimate level if you live apart?"

Many of our typical solutions revolve around avoiding conflict, hassles, and confrontations instead of resolving them. Unfortunately, avoiding an issue almost always means perpetuating the conflict.

Unresolved conflict does not go away, it persists.

In reality, avoidance translates into giving permission to the difficult people in our lives to continue to manipulate to get their needs met. Assertive people do not avoid issues, but work proactively to solve them.

IT SOUNDS AS THOUGH SOME PEOPLE HAVE HAD LITTLE EXPERIENCE WITH ASSERTIVE COMMUNICATION AND BEHAVIOR.

In reality, many people have *never* learned to communicate assertively, and the people who have are often so frustrated trying to deal with the games and manipulation of others that they may end up resorting to those same negative techniques and abandon their more assertive attempts. The fact remains, however, *if* we want to neutralize difficult people, then we must absolutely commit to communicating assertively. That requires us to think, plan, and respond to others without gimmicks, tricks, intimidation, or guilt. The first problem is that very few of us plan our communications. We tend to simply react and speak without much thought. We seldom weigh our choices (if we even remember or admit that we have a choice), or consider redefining our skills. Why? Because most people consider communicating to be an event—not a process. "Thinking and planning sounds like work," you say. Right! Communicating assertively *is* work because assertiveness does not come naturally for most of us. It takes practice not to respond automatically using our old childhood repertoire of phrases, arguments, and excuses that involve manipulation and game playing.

DO YOU MEAN THAT I HAVE TO PLAN OUT EVERYTHING I'M GOING TO SAY?

Yes. Most people tend to view communication as something that just happens rather than a learned skill. Small talk may just happen without thinking, but communicating with forthrightness, honesty, and resolve is definitely a learned skill that requires considerable practice. Communication is the key to all of our relationships, and because we are social creatures, good relationships are necessary to our well-being. Poor communication is, without a doubt, one of the primary causes of failed relationships. Unfortunately, this means most people are *choosing* to communicate in one of the nonassertive styles:

aggressive, passive, or passive-aggressive, which invariably leads to an unhealthy relationship or a breakdown of a relationship altogether.

ARE YOU SAYING THAT I CANNOT GET MY NEEDS MET IN A RELATIONSHIP IF I USE ONE OF THE NONASSERTIVE COMMUNICATION STYLES?

In the short term, the three nonassertive styles of communication may be undeniably effective in getting your needs met, as you will see in the chapters ahead. In the long term, those communication strategies literally kill relationships and, thus, they will undermine every attempt you make to bring the relationship to a higher, healthier level. Mistrust, put-downs, silence, intimidation, and coercion are not the keys to healthy relationships. So, although difficult people appear to get their way for the time being, the people around them are usually plotting to escape the relationship altogether or to seek revenge. Eventually, people who view life as win/lose inevitably lose everything—including the people they love and the job they covet.

WHAT HAPPENS WHEN WE CHOOSE TO BEHAVE ASSERTIVELY IN OUR RELATIONSHIPS?

Only the assertive person has relationships that sustain rather than drain. Without a doubt, assertive behavior is the best way to interact with everyone because assertiveness is the only way we can get our needs met consistently and, at the same time, maintain mutually respectful, healthy relationships. When we learn to behave assertively, many benefits flood our lives. For instance, we lose the resentment we feel toward those who try to manipulate and intimidate us. We create relationships that satisfy our needs without compromising our integrity. When we begin to assert ourselves, we will find that others respect us more and, at the same time, our own self-respect is heightened. Whenever you are tempted to give in, give out, or give up to a difficult person, please remember:

Difficult people only respect people who have
the confidence to stand up for themselves.

In fact, giving in to or ignoring difficult behavior will only insure that it occurs more frequently because the difficult person has now identified you as a person who will accept, even reward, unacceptable behavior. Difficult people follow a pattern. They will first try to manipulate you through hurt or anger. If you give in, they will lose respect for you and begin to manipulate you even more. You will then give in more quickly, trying desperately to salvage the relationship and make things better. They lose even more respect and the pattern continues. If this process continues for very long, some form of physical, verbal, or emotional abuse will probably begin to occur. Thus, we begin a vicious cycle—a cycle, however, that we can break with our determination to respond and communicate assertively. Now, with all of this talk about the liberating power of assertiveness, I need to add one important caveat:

Warning: Difficult people will *not* like to be treated assertively *at first* because they will no longer be getting their way.

If you are hoping your problems with difficult people will be over immediately upon becoming assertive, you will be sorely disappointed. Remember, we said assertiveness is the most effective communication style over time. It took a long time for us to train difficult people to treat us poorly, and it will take considerable time to retrain them. If they are used to whining, yelling, cajoling, intimidating, or coercing to get you to react to their needs, they will not suddenly be delighted with your new, forthright, assertive responses. They are not likely to say, "Thank you so much for asserting yourself when I try to manipulate you. You have forced me to reconsider my behavior and learn to be more assertive myself. I'm glad we can now communicate together in a mature and up-front way." Remember, assertiveness is their biggest enemy and their worst nightmare because it means that you have finally figured them out and, even more important, you are refusing to be swayed by their manipulative attempts. In fact, you are now holding them accountable for their own behavior—exactly what they do not want. Most difficult people are not expecting this assertive reaction, so you had better be prepared for some trying times with the difficult person when you first become assertive. For instance:

- Asserting yourself with an employer who is used to you working overtime, missing lunch, accepting angry criticism and attacks, may earn you the label of an insubordinate.
- Asserting yourself with a parent who has become comfortable with your total compliance and willingness to let guilt cause you to give in may cause them to declare, "You don't love me anymore."
- Asserting yourself with a child who loves the control they have over you in terms of clothes, curfew, or chores may cause them to yell, "You're mean and you don't care about me. I hate you."

Do you see what difficult people are hoping to accomplish by attacking you? They are confident that by using their old standbys, hurt and anger, they can once again convince you to throw your hands up in defeat and go back to the good old days. Those were the days when they usually got their way and you accommodated by giving in to them in response to their manipulations.

In other words, assertiveness is no quick fix. Not only will it take a lot of practice to communicate assertively, it will also take considerable patience and time before major changes will begin to occur in the relationship. You need to know that:

Assertive action may mean that things
get worse before they get better!

I TRIED TO BE ASSERTIVE ONCE
AND IT DID NOT WORK

Once? Of course it did not work! The difficult person is not going to cave in and be perfectly nice after your first try. Do not ever underestimate them. They think they have you figured out. Your nemesis will probably pull out the big guns when their ploys no longer work. They will attempt to cry more, yell louder, or pout longer. There may even come a time when the difficult person delivers an ultimatum like "Stop acting this way. Go back to the way it was or the relationship is over!" Remember, "acting this way" means you are not responding to their manipulations and giving in to their every whim.

Sadly enough, there are many difficult people so locked into the game of manipulation, so intent on getting their way and so sure they are right, that they would rather dissolve the relationship than meet you half way and work on raising your communication to a new and honest level. "Why even bother?" you may ask. "I'm unhappy in the relationship now, why would I willingly communicate in a way that might make it worse for awhile, or perhaps end the relationship altogether?"

Before you ask yourself that question, let me ask you something very important. Do you *really* want this relationship to be better? If you do, then using short-term strategies to avoid the problem, making you feel good momentarily is not the answer. You may be creating what appears to be a tolerable, peaceful existence, but at what price? Your sanity? Your feeling of safety? Your health and well-being? Your self-respect? Self-respect is the true key to developing and maintaining healthy relationships.

Remember what is stated in chapter 1: *You will be treated exactly as you allow yourself to be treated.*

If you are a person who is constantly surrounded by difficult people, then take a look at how you feel about yourself. Everyone has a few difficult people here and there throughout their life, but if it seems as though almost everyone you know treats you badly, then perhaps others are simply reflecting your own negative feelings about yourself.

Our relationships with others only mirror
our relationship with ourselves.

IT SOUNDS LIKE IT TAKES A LOT OF SELF-CONFIDENCE TO COMMUNICATE ASSERTIVELY.

Yes, it does. Often, people begin therapy by saying, "My problem is I lack the self-esteem to tell others how I really feel." Let's begin by getting rid of the myth that some people have self-esteem and others do not. We all have self-esteem, just as we all have a mind, heart, and body. But, some of us do not take the time to help our emotional part (which includes our self-esteem, self-respect, and

confidence) stay in shape. As adults, we must continue to work and develop our self-esteem, much like building up our muscles to tone our body and learning new skills to keep our minds alert. When people would tell me in therapy, "I make such self-destructive, stupid decisions because my self-esteem is low," I would always respond emphatically, "No! Your self-esteem is low *because* you are making stupid, self-destructive choices."

Developing self-esteem takes work—hard work. Having confidence in ourselves takes practice and occurs when we consistently strive to make healthy, ethical choices in our lives. The positive feelings we get as a result of these good choices begin to accumulate, and, over time, our self-esteem is toned and fit.

> Self-esteem develops when we consistently strive
> to make healthy, fair, and ethical choices.

When we make poor choices that are not good for ourselves and others, we generally experience feelings that are not comfortable or pleasant (shame, sadness, etc.). Our self-esteem and confidence in our abilities may drop, and then we have to strive to make better choices to build it back up, much like putting on a few pounds after the holiday season and reconfirming our fitness plan soon after.

Self-esteem and a positive, healthy emotional outlook is developed because constant attention is paid to that emotional part of us, just as a healthy physical body is developed by paying constant attention to our diet and exercise. No one would expect to be physically healthy without hard work, so why would we expect to be emotionally healthy without an equal investment of time and energy? The exercises that will keep our self-esteem toned and fit are making consistent choices that are fair, ethical, and healthy. One by one, choice by choice, our self-esteem is firmed and toned.

IF SELF-ESTEEM IS DEVELOPED BY MAKING GOOD CHOICES, WHAT HAPPENS TO CHILDREN WHO OFTEN HAVE NO CHOICE ABOUT WHAT THEY DO OR WHAT HAPPENS TO THEM?

Children, indeed, are different because they are dependent and thus limited in their choices. They usually cannot choose with whom they live, where they go to school, or who their teachers are. Instead, their self-esteem is generally reflected by the choices other people (especially their teachers, caretakers, and friends) make in terms of modeling behavior and setting fair, legal, and ethical standards for them to witness and emulate. If the adults in their lives make poor choices involving manipulation, threats, abuse, neglect, or intimidation, children can easily lose important confidence in themselves. That is why it is so important that all children have the best role models possible, so that they can learn by example not only how to treat others respectfully, but how they should expect (and demand) to be treated in return. In my book, *Self-Esteem and the Six-Second Secret*, I discuss in detail how parents and teachers can be effective role models and teach their children and students to respect themselves and others, thus helping children develop the high self-esteem needed to be assertive adults.

This is not to excuse a child's illegal behavior. Unfortunately, we are in a world today where children are committing dangerous, self-destructive, and even horrifying acts. These children must accept the consequences of their actions. It is even more vital now that we work together—community, church, school, and home—to ensure that each child has the best opportunity possible to be in the presence of functional, healthy adults, so they can learn how to love, respect, and care for other people.

FOR ADULTS WHO DID NOT RECEIVE GOOD MESSAGES ABOUT ASSERTIVENESS, CONFLICT RESOLUTION AND SELF-RESPECT WHEN THEY WERE CHILDREN, WILL IT BE MORE DIFFICULT FOR THEM TO COMMUNICATE IN A POSITIVE, HEALTHY WAY LATER IN LIFE?

Yes, it will be difficult unless they make a conscious decision to change old patterns and communication styles in order to ensure that their relationships are as healthy as possible. At first, it may be hard to overcome some of the negative messages and feelings that accumulated throughout their childhood and replace them with positive, healthy ones. It may be difficult to think of themselves, perhaps, as worthwhile beings who deserve to be treated with respect and dignity. It may be difficult to eliminate some of the prejudices that keep them from treating others respectfully. It may even be difficult to communicate assertively and avoid using the manipulation techniques that have worked so well in the past, and replace them with nondefensive, open, and honest dialogue. None of these positive steps and changes, however, will be as difficult as continuing to deal with people and situations in the same way they have been in the past, only to discover that most of their relationships are hurtful, nonproductive, and unfulfilling.

Please note that although it may be more difficult for an adult who did not receive the valuable, positive messages and role modeling to be assertive, assertiveness is still a *choice* they have at their disposal. For them, however, it will just require more conscious effort.

When people in counseling would tell me about their dysfunctional childhood, the caregivers who did not love them or the things that had been lacking, I would listen, understand, and give them some direction so they could sort through the sadness and anger. Then, I would ask them, "Now what?" They would respond, "What do you mean?" and I would answer firmly, "So now, knowing what you know and the mistakes and weaknesses of some people in your life, what are *you* now going to do to change these patterns and create a new, positive life for yourself?"

Sometimes, they would be stunned because many of them had spent weeks, even years of their lives looking back and constantly focusing on all the bad, unfortunate things that had happened to them. If someone is always reliving the sordid, unhappy, or unloving past, it is almost impossible for them to look ahead to a brighter future. Also, their unhealthy past had given them an excuse that they often used to explain away the problems in their present life involving their attitudes, choices, and relationships. In other words, they had allowed their past to give them permission to play the part of the victim. As long as someone considers themselves a victim they do not feel required to accept responsibility for their own choices and they can continue to go through life saying, "It's not my fault!"

SO WHAT DO I NEED TO DO FIRST SO I CAN DEAL WITH DIFFICULT PEOPLE MORE ASSERTIVELY?

Do a personal self-esteem inventory.

- Do you think you are important?
- Do you value yourself?
- Do you appreciate your worth as a person?
- Do you believe you deserve to be treated with respect?

These are tough but important questions that must be answered before you even attempt to successfully deal with other people. Without the inner commitment and belief that you deserve to be communicated to and treated with respect, love, honesty, and compassion, you will not be able to change the dynamics in your most stressful relationships. First, it will be difficult, if not impossible, for you to use assertive communication techniques. Assertiveness requires more than just words. The words must reflect a belief you have in yourself that radiates through your voice, gestures, tone, attitude, and body language that says, "I am a worthy person and I *will* be treated respectfully." You can yell, "I don't deserve this!" over and over, but difficult people are masters at reading the deeper message and quickly determining whether you will back up your words with assertive action.

I AM AFRAID THAT IF I DEMAND RESPECT AND BECOME MORE ASSERTIVE, THE RELATIONSHIP MIGHT END. IS THIS TRUE?

Yes, it could happen. It takes courage to risk a relationship, but assertive people must be willing not only to risk it, but perhaps to end it and move on. We must mean what we say, and say what we mean. We need to believe, without a doubt, that we are capable people who can get another job, find another friend, or become partners in another significant relationship. In other words, assertive people believe in no uncertain terms that there is life—quality life—beyond bad relationships. Assertive people are not afraid of being alone because they have already developed a comfortable, supportive relationship with themselves.

Separating without any attempt to communicate or without working to resolve an issue is avoidance. However, believing in yourself enough to leave a situation or relationship where abuse or a lack of respect exists, or attempts to communicate assertively do not work, is a different story. Sometimes, a partner in an abusive, addictive relationship would tell me, "But, I don't want to be a quitter."

It is *not* quitting to have the courage and self-respect
to sever an abusive or addictive relationship.

Sometimes being assertive is knowing when it is imperative to our well-being and self-respect to disengage.

Self-respect: where assertiveness begins and manipulation ends.

WHAT ARE MY CHOICES IF I AM IN A RELATIONSHIP WITH A DIFFICULT PERSON?

As our self-esteem and confidence increase as a result of making healthy, ethical decisions, we can effectively move into the assertive mode and start to stand up to difficult people in earnest. Basically, there are three choices in any difficult relationship.

1. *Accept the relationship as it is, recognizing that the difficult person will not change just because you want them to.* After reading this book, some of you may decide that you honestly do not want to go through the work and dedication it takes to become an assertive communicator and may not want to risk changing or ending the relationship. Some of you may decide that the situation is not bad enough to warrant the time and energy needed to improve things. If this is your choice, be aware that their behavior toward you will probably worsen because you are continuing to play an important part and you are giving them permission to treat you disrespectfully.

2. *You can stay in the relationship and try to change the difficult person rather than changing yourself.* If this is your choice, please be aware of the futility of trying to change anyone. Others do not change their behaviors simply because we want them to. People change because they personally have decided it is to their own best advantage. In fact, our acceptance of their unacceptable behavior may be exactly the reason why it continues. The term *codependence* means a situation where a person not only allows unacceptable behavior, but participates in the process. That means if you stay in the relationship and try to change the difficult person, you will probably become a manipulative person yourself. The relationship will generally get worse, and you may even become what you hate about the other person. There is no doubt that your self-esteem will plummet as you continue to make choices that are unhealthy.

3. *You decide you cannot accept the situation as is.* You know that the difficult person will not choose to change as long as you continue to play your part in this "drama of life." You decide to learn new techniques and skills that will allow you to be in control of yourself so that you can react and begin to respond assertively to their manipulations. You let the difficult person know in an assertive way what you need and expect.

If you choose the third option, you must begin to integrate assertive communication and behavior into every aspect of the relationship. You should prepare yourself to weather the storm if they react negatively to your commitment and hold them accountable for their negative behavior. You must be confident that there is a good chance that they will sense your determination to change the relationship in a positive way and will begin to respond to your assertive lead. As you continue to make healthy choices concerning yourself and your relationship with them, your self-esteem is heightened. And, as your confidence grows, assertiveness becomes second nature. At this point, you are prepared for whatever may happen. If they choose to work on the relationship for the mutual benefit of you both, then you can begin again to trust one another. But, if they refuse to stop their hurtful, inappropriate, or destructive behavior toward you, you are prepared to sever the relationship if it means compromising your self-respect.

WHAT SHOULD I EXPECT MIGHT HAPPEN IF I CHOOSE THE THIRD OPTION, TO BE MORE ASSERTIVE AND LET THE DIFFICULT PERSON KNOW WHAT I NEED AND EXPECT?

If you choose the third option, you must realize that by changing yourself and becoming assertive, one thing is almost certain: The difficult person will probably go into overdrive and push harder to bring back the "old" you. However, if you persevere and continue to state your needs, boundaries, and expectations, communicate honestly and stay committed, insisting that you be treated fairly and respectfully, one of the following two things will happen:

1. The difficult person will respond to your lead. They will begin to explore new ways of communicating because the old ones are no longer getting their needs met. They will manipulate less and begin to communicate more openly, or

2. The difficult person will refuse to change and issue an ultimatum such as, "Stop this or we're through." Now we are back to the question: How do you feel you deserve to be treated? Are you willing to continue a relationship where the other person has made it clear that he or she will not change their behavior or attitude toward you? Can you continue to sustain the relationship and keep your self-respect intact? These are tough questions, but ones you must answer.

IT SOUNDS LIKE INSISTING ON A QUALITY LIFE WITH QUALITY RELATIONSHIPS INVOLVES A CERTAIN AMOUNT OF RISK.

Yes, it does. It always has. Many people are very uncomfortable taking risks, which is exactly what the difficult person hopes. Difficult people are counting on the fact that we are not willing to risk the relationship in return for our self-respect. The good news is that it has been my experience that most difficult people are bluffing, and they usually begin to respond more positively if we continue to use our assertive skills.

As long as you stay determined, communicate honestly while keeping in mind their needs as well as yours, and work hard to negotiate win/win solutions, difficult people will usually meet the challenge. In fact, many difficult people are excellent mediators, debaters, and problem solvers. It is just that they have never had a need to use those skills because they have spent years engaging in successful manipulative behaviors. The truth is, negotiation takes longer than coercion or intimidation. Difficult people choose the most expedient solution. Chances are good that you will start seeing some exciting evidence of assertiveness at work soon after the initial period during which the situation gets worse before it gets better.

WHAT DO I DO WITH THOSE FEW DIFFICULT PEOPLE WHO WILL ABSOLUTELY, UNEQUIVOCALLY REFUSE TO WORK WITH ME AND COMMIT TO AN OPEN, HONEST, AND ASSERTIVE RELATIONSHIP?

Their message to you is loud and clear: "I insist on being in total control. I will not change how I talk to you or treat you. I will not learn to communicate openly, and I will continue to use manipulation." Their ultimatum is nonnegotiable. They are saying, "Either revert to the way we used to communicate where you did exactly what I wanted and put up with my anger [abuse, sarcasm, hurt feelings, intimidation, betrayal, etc.], or we're through!" There should be no misunderstanding here. The enemy is armed and ready for battle. The negotiations are off! They will only allow one winner in this relationship. If you receive this threat, you have only the following two choices:

1. ***You can give in, stay in the relationship as is, and continue to be manipulated.*** If this is your choice, that is fine, but do not complain about them . . . ever again! You are now fully aware of what is going on. You know without a doubt that their behavior will probably continue forever and get worse as soon as they realize you will no longer insist on being treated respectfully. In fact, you have now become a willing participant (and they know it). It is no longer their fault—you cannot blame them. You are not a victim. Victims are never willing and have *not* made a conscious choice to be treated badly. You *are* willing and have made a *choice.* Once you have made this choice, it is time to move on and accommodate the choices you have made, knowing that your self-respect is being wagered on this relationship.

2. ***You can decide, "No more."*** Now that you have insight and knowledge into the game and finally understand that this person is *not* going to change, you can refuse to play your part in the dysfunctional relationship ever again. You realize that there is nothing more you can do. You have communicated as openly and manipulation-free as you can. They *choose* not to respond. They *refuse* to work it out. You have had a taste of assertiveness, however, and you love it. You have heard yourself state your needs clearly. You have watched yourself refuse to accept abuse or mistreatment. You have noticed that you feel in control of your life. You have recognized that it is not you who has the problem, and you realize that you cannot change or fix the other person. You are proud of yourself and your commitment to being treated fairly and with dignity. You simply cannot go back to the way you were treated before. You are ready to move on, find another job that you love, tell the grown children it is time to find a place of their own, dissolve a friendship that has out-lasted its usefulness, or leave a significant other or spouse who has not truly loved or supported you for years. Begin to live your life without the stress, anger, and frustration that comes with manipulation.

You are ready to find other relationships where your assertiveness is admired, applauded, and appreciated. Does this sound wonderful? You bet! Now it is time to stay assertive and use those techniques in your daily life. Being assertive means being effective at neutralizing the three communication styles identified earlier: aggressive, passive, and passive-aggressive. The following chapters will take a look at each of these styles in more depth and describe how you can deal with each of the other styles more assertively. If you will take to heart the lessons in the next three chapters, you may be on your way to saying good-bye to the difficult people in your life. So, let's go inside the personality control centers of several difficult people and see just what makes them tick so we can learn how to act and react to their games and manipulations.

Summary

- Assertiveness is the *only* communication style that will allow us to have a healthy relationship with the people in our lives.
- When we are assertive we choose to handle ourselves, our reactions, our relationships, and stressful situations in a healthy, responsible, and nonmanipulative manner.
- Communication is a learned skill.
- You will be treated exactly as you feel you deserve to be treated.
- We must model assertive communication to our children so they can learn to handle conflict and sustain healthy relationships.
- Each of us is responsible for our behavior even if negative things happened to us as a child.
- Our relationships with others only mirrors our relationship with ourselves.
- Self-esteem develops when we consistently strive to make healthy, fair, and ethical choices.
- Difficult people only respect people who have the confidence to stand up for themselves.
- It is *not* quitting to have the courage and self-respect to sever an abusive or addictive relationship.

Take Action

- Look closely at the times your family or friends are assertive. How do you react? Doesn't it feel good to be with someone who is upfront, honest, and cooperative?
- Think about the times when you are not assertive. What other communication style(s) do you most often use? Does it work? Are you rewarded for your nonassertive behavior?
- Try to be assertive at the times you might use another communication style. Do others react more positively toward you?

THE AGGRESSIVE PERSONALITY

Manipulation Through Hurt and Anger

When we hear the word *aggressive*, we tend to think of people who are overbearing, powerful, and intimidating. We imagine people who will stop at nothing and who may even use physical force to get their way. Football players are aggressive. Soldiers are aggressive. Bank robbers are aggressive. But, I would like to expand *aggression* to include any interaction where one fails to acknowledge another person's rights, needs, and/or concerns. The aggressive personality is a person whose only concern is seeing that their needs get met regardless of the methods used or the consequences of their actions. Compromise, discussion, and mediation are not in their vocabulary. Believe me, as you will see in this chapter, one does not have to be physically intimidating to qualify as aggressive. After all, whining, crying, complaining, and hurting another's feelings can be as manipulative as yelling, threatening, or intimidating another person. If we are honest, most of us will admit that we have each used aggressive techniques and behaviors a time or two (maybe more?) in our own lives. There are, however, people who use the aggressive style as their most common communication technique.

In the game called "getting our needs met," aggressives are masters. Relationships are seldom peaceful, either personally or professionally. The aggressive considers life a competitive sport and is constantly searching for opponents to conquer. "I win, you lose," is their sacred creed. As stated in chapter 2, aggressives do not even attempt to negotiate but instead focus on manipulation and intimidation, which explains why they are so difficult and tiring to be around. We must be on constant guard when we are with them lest we find ourselves out of the game altogether.

WHY ARE THERE SOME PEOPLE WHO USE AGGRESSIVE AS THEIR MAIN STYLE OF COMMUNICATION, WHEREAS OTHERS SEEM BETTER AT PROBLEM SOLVING, MEDIATING, LISTENING, AND WORKING TOGETHER COOPERATIVELY?

To answer that, we again have to look back at our childhood experiences. At an early age, our subconscious began to play an important role in our lives. Remember, the subconscious is a very potent part of our psychological make-up: It is dedicated to seeing that we get what we want. As we discussed before, our subconscious consists of a very efficient information storage capacity that remembers meticulously what actions get specific results. Our subconscious can call up that data instantly when it feels our needs or desires are being thwarted. Unfortunately, our subconscious often acts with little or no thought—this is called a reaction. However, the good news is we can usually override these thoughts and consciously *choose* new and different patterns of communication and behaviors. This reprogramming may take considerable time and energy because erasing or overlooking "old tapes" (messages heard so often that one begins to repeat them) requires a thorough understanding of how and why we feel, think, and communicate the way we do.

Self-evaluation is difficult, and it is often easier to just say and do what we have always done rather than change. Conscious decisions almost always take more thought and planning. When people say, "I can't help acting this way," or "Well, that's just who I am," they are allowing themselves to act and react without thinking about the consequences rather than taking conscious responsibility for weighing their choices and taking charge.

WHY ARE *HURT* AND *ANGER* SO EFFECTIVE WHEN ONE IS USING THE AGGRESSIVE STYLE OF COMMUNICATION?

The two emotions used most frequently to manipulate others into giving us what we want are hurt and anger. These two emotions

form a simple but powerful arsenal from which we can pull an end-
less number of manipulative weapons that can weaken and eliminate opposition to our needs. The truth is that communication does
not need to get much more complex than this because these two
ploys are remarkably effective—effective enough in most cases to
become our default strategies whenever (even as adults) we feel that
our needs are not getting met. In fact, once you learn to watch for
them, you will soon discover that almost every difficult person you
come in contact with is using one of these two techniques to get their
way.

Think of people who use hurt as a tool to get us to cave in to their
demands: whiners, complainers, mopers, and of course, the "victims." These are the people who want us to feel responsible for them
and their situation so we will give in to their needs.

A good point to remember is:

---

*We are responsible to people, but we
are not responsible for people.*

People who use anger also come to mind. They threaten, yell,
scream, slam doors, give "killer" looks, use sarcasm, put-downs, and
belittling statements. Their objective is to make us feel powerless so
we will give in to their demands.

I HAVE FELT HURT AND ANGRY BEFORE. ARE YOU SAYING I SHOULD NOT HAVE THOSE FEELINGS OR WHEN I DO, I AM BEING MANIPULATIVE?

Not at all. When I use the terms *hurt* and *anger*, most of you will
immediately think of your own valid experiences where you felt
hurt or angry, such as the pain of being betrayed, the grief experienced over a loss, or the response to being attacked or belittled. In
those cases and many others, hurt and anger are legitimate responses
to external events. Those emotions are not what I am talking about
here. Rather, I am talking about using (not feeling) these two emotions to manipulate a response from another person.

When someone is being manipulative, they either use hurt to make a person feel guilty or they use anger to make someone feel afraid, powerless, or inadequate.

Aggressives know that many people will respond to the ensuing feelings of guilt produced by their hurt or feelings of powerlessness or fear produced by their anger, by giving in to them. Thus, we witness the cycle of manipulation.

HOW CAN WE KNOW WHEN SOMEONE IS USING HURT OR ANGER TO BE MANIPULATIVE OR WHEN THOSE FEELINGS AND EMOTIONS ARE MEANINGFUL AND APPROPRIATE?

One of the easiest cues is to check out our own feelings when confronted with another's hurt or anger. When someone is manipulating us using hurt or anger, their ultimate goal is for us to feel guilty, insecure, afraid, or inadequate. However, when these emotions are used appropriately, we feel empathy for the other person's anger, distress, or sorrow, but we do not internalize or accept responsibility for their feelings or situation nor do we experience negative feelings about ourselves.

WHY WOULD SOMEONE WANT US TO FEEL GUILTY OR AFRAID?

Think back to your own experiences when dealing with feelings of guilt and intimidation. Our first response to both guilt and fear is usually to doubt ourselves and our choices and to do everything possible to get rid of those feelings. It works like this: If we feel guilty, then perhaps (we surmise) we have done something wrong; therefore, we will want to change our behavior, thoughts, attitudes, or beliefs in order to feel better about ourselves again. If we feel afraid and powerless, then we may do whatever is necessary for us to feel in control again. If someone can produce feelings of guilt or fear in us as a result of manipulation though hurt or anger, then we will usually try every response we can think of to eliminate those negative feelings. To make matters worse, both fear and guilt can (and often do), manifest themselves as physical sensations, symptoms, or even illnesses that are uncomfortable, destructive, or painful. No wonder, then, that hurt and anger often trigger an instant knee-jerk reaction in us whereby we change our minds or our behavior in order to regain our sense of well-being. The difficult person is betting that we will give in to them in order to feel better about ourselves.

On the other hand, when someone expresses the emotions of hurt and anger appropriately, they do not elicit the same instant reaction in us to change ourselves in order to regain our self-confidence. Instead, we feel comfortable responding with active listening, some helpful advice, a sympathetic ear, or an offer of help without assuming responsibility.

SO WHEN DO PEOPLE BEGIN TO USE MANIPULATIVE BEHAVIOR ON OTHERS?

We begin using manipulative behavior sooner than you think. Children go through stages when they try all sorts of devious behaviors to try to convince their parents to give them what they want. In many cases, the child will identify one parent to fire on with both barrels while showing far more restraint around the other parent. Most children are already smart and devious enough by the ages of 3 or 4 to try to pit mom and dad (or whomever the caregivers may be) against each other. In this way, they can even the odds so that it is not two against one. Mom and dad united could be a formidable, if not impossible, adversary, so the child learns quickly to focus his or her manipulative tricks on one parent. The other parent may seldom witness the full range of the child's ability to whine, scream, and pout.

HOW DO CHILDREN IDENTIFY WHICH PARENT TO "TARGET" FOR THEIR MANIPULATIVE BEHAVIOR?

Most children are intuitive enough to focus on the parent they believe to be more susceptible to either hurt or anger. Often, one parent wants peace and harmony at all costs and will give in, ignore, rationalize, make excuses for, reward, or make deals with the difficult child. The other parent may be less inclined to make such deals and may try instead to set limits, give consequences, or invoke discipline in order to teach the child that certain behavior is not acceptable. It is readily apparent to the child which parent will give in and allow the limits and boundaries to be stretched, and that information is dutifully filed away by the child's subconscious. Later in life, this information will be retrieved to help them identify which family members, friends, coworkers, and employers are also easy targets for their manipulative behaviors.

It is not uncommon for parents to hold contradictory views on how to handle a child's negative behavior. Sadly, it is often the parent who wants to set limits who backs down and gives in to the parent who wants to keep the peace at any price. In fact, discipline-minded parents often remove themselves from the entire realm of discipline, having learned from experience what happens when they try to step in: the sympathetic, indulgent parent rushes to the child's defense. At that point, the two against one odds are in the child's favor. The discipline-minded parent, whose strategy is the one that would eventually produce the least manipulative child, learns instead to turn the other way, thus contributing to the emergence of an aggressive and manipulative personality.

To clarify, by *discipline-minded* I am not talking about a parent who is overly strict, controlling, punitive, or one who resorts to any form of verbal, emotional, or physical abuse as a discipline tool. In such cases, the sympathetic parent is the child's only advocate. Instead, I am talking about a parent who, in a nonabusive, assertive way, tries to set firm limits and establish fair and reasonable consequences for unacceptable behavior and whose efforts are rendered useless by a too-lenient parent.

To reiterate, even in early childhood all children are learning what they need to do to get what they want. And what do they want? They want the same thing difficult adults want: They want to do their own thing, in their own time, in their own way, without any interference.

HOW DOES A CHILD USE HURT OR ANGER TO MANIPULATE?

Let's take a look at 5-year-old Diane and her mom. Mom is tired at the end of a long, busy day and still has dinner to cook, homework to assist, and baths to give. She is preparing dinner, which will be ready at 6 p.m. Diane walks into the kitchen at 5:30 p.m. and asks for a cookie. The typical response would be, "No, a cookie will spoil your appetite. Wait for dinner in 30 minutes."

At this point, Diane has two choices. She can accept "no" as an answer or try another approach and begin experimenting with some manipulative behaviors to see what might work on her mom to get her the cookie.

If Diane pouts, whines, cries, and tries to make her mom feel guilty, she has moved into behaviors using hurt to manipulate. Does Diane consciously know what she is doing? Well, yes and no. She could not put into words that she is using behaviors that will produce a feeling of guilt (most adults could not even verbalize that), but she *does* know she wants the cookie and "no" was not an acceptable answer. Therefore, she is using every technique possible to change Mom's mind in order to get her way. The scenario might sound like the following:

Diane says, "But Mommmm . . . this morning you had to go to work early and you forgot my lunch money. That's okay because Amy's mom doesn't work and she always puts a little extra in Amy's lunch in case you forget to feed me. (Do you see the guilt beginning to creep up in Mom?) We never make homemade cookies anymore and you hardly even have time to go to the store to buy snacks. Please . . . just one cookie?"

If Diane's whining works, and she succeeds in making Mom feel guilty, then Mom will most likely do almost anything to get rid of that feeling. The easiest way to eliminate guilt, in this case, is to go to the pantry and get Diane a cookie. What happens when Diane gets her way? Diane wipes away her tears and perks up. Mom feels better because the guilt is gone. Is everyone happy? Well, it would appear so for the present. Mom does not have to feel like a "bad" mother and Diane is enjoying her cookie. The problem, however, is that Diane has just learned a sad, but true lesson about the way life works: Make someone feel bad and you will be rewarded!

When she had asked for a cookie in an assertive, respectful way, she did not push any guilt buttons and her demands were *not* met. But, when she cried and whined, a cookie appeared in her hand! Diane will store this valuable piece of communication information away to pull out the next time someone says no. Her subconscious has now filed away information that says "whining, crying, and making Mom feel bad works! I get what I want." As you can see, we do indeed train and reward people when they use manipulative techniques. No wonder there are so many difficult personalities for us to deal with.

When we reward negative and manipulative
behavior, that behavior will occur again.

Now, let us suppose for a moment that *hurt* did not work. Diane tried and failed because Mom did not fall for it. Mom calmly said,

"Well, Diane, you can pout and cry, but it's not going to change my mind. No cookie until after dinner." (Notice: This was said very assertively. Mom did not respond by using hurt or anger herself.)

If Diane consistently hears assertive responses, she will soon learn a different lesson and file away the information that using hurt is *not* effective. Her attempts to manipulate were *not* rewarded and she did *not* get her needs met. Chances are, she will seldom resort to this tactic in other situations later in life.

Diane may now try another manipulative technique: anger. She may criticize, attack, scream, yell, stomp, or throw a tantrum. Her goal is to intimidate her mother. The scenario might work like the following:

> Diane yells, "Fine! I hate you. I wish I had Amy's mom. You never pay attention to me any more since you've started working. If my brother wanted a cookie, I bet you'd give him one. You've always liked him better than me."

How will some parents feel after listening to this routine? Inadequate? Unfit? Uncaring? Willing to do anything to get rid of those feelings? Even though at a conscious level Mom knows Diane has plenty to eat every day, her daughter's act (and it is an act) may succeed. It will definitely succeed if Mom already feels badly and questions her adequacy as a parent. By the time Diane finishes her tantrum, her mom may begin to criticize herself: "Diane's right—I'm away too much. I work too hard. Amy's mom cares more—she's always there. How could I forget her lunch? I was too busy to go to the store—how could I do that? What's wrong with me? Why can't I do a better job? It's my fault she's hungry. Poor little thing."

Diane's guilt barrage will also succeed if Mom is simply tired and does not want a hassle. Mom may think to herself, "I've heard people whining all day. I'm exhausted. If I say no, she won't stop. I simply can't deal with this now. One cookie won't hurt this once—anything to put an end to her whining and tantrums!"

Either way, Diane wins, walks away with the cookie and the aggressive behavior becomes reinforced. Diane's mom may feel better because the guilt, fear, or hassle is over; however, we just taught a child one of the most unforgettable and unfortunate lessons in the world:

> Ask for something with respect and you do not
> get it, but use manipulation and you win.

That lesson basically sums up the aggressive personality's main strategy: to win no matter what the cost, even if it means making someone else feel bad, sad, or inadequate. Aggressive people definitely see others as their adversaries—people standing in the way of them getting what they want. You are in the way, so you must be dealt with and rendered defenseless to the difficult person. That means they must control you. This is the battle they are constantly waging, and why every encounter with them feels like such a struggle.

> Difficult people are in a war for control,
> and they will go to any length to win.

Hopefully, Mom can model good assertive communication which would be a far better lesson for Diane. Mom should say, "Diane! That behavior and tone of voice is unacceptable. There will be no cookie before dinner and now there won't be one after dinner either. That is not how we talk to one another in this house."

WHY IS GUILT SUCH A POWERFUL MANIPULATOR?

People who use hurt to manipulate intend to produce big-time guilt.

> Guilt is one of the most debilitating emotions we can feel
> because it causes us to doubt ourselves and our decisions,
> and, as a result, we feel unworthy and inadequate.

Guilt is incredibly powerful because it works at a subconscious level. It is the perfect saboteur.

First, people who use guilt as a way of controlling others are always keeping score. Many times you do not even know you have run up an account with them, but with a "guilt producer," no good deed of theirs goes unrecorded. With them there are no random acts of kindness. Everything they do for you goes into the account book, and you will be expected to pay them back. Have you ever tried to assertively say "no" to someone, only to have them act hurt and list all the things they have done for you in the past? Parents can be great at this. I call this the "Litany of Sacrifice." It goes like this:

> "Fine, John. I do so much for you, and you won't even rake the yard without that attitude of yours. Do you think money grows on trees? I cook, clean, drive you to soccer. All I ask of you is one thing and you can't even help me without complaining."

Let's be honest. Rather than saying assertively, "John, I need you to rake the yard. I know you'd rather be at the movies, but this needs to be done now, before dinner," the parent employs hurt, and tries to make John feel guilty. The theory is if John feels like a bad, unappreciative son, he will gladly jump at the opportunity to help.

Second, guilt can create symptoms that literally make us feel ill—both physically and psychologically. When we face any form of bacteria or virus, our bodies immediately try to protect us—to rush to our rescue with antibodies to fight the infection. It is the same with the guilt virus. It stimulates self-doubt so that we find ourselves going over and over our past actions: What did we do? What didn't we do? What should we have done or said? When held up by someone's guilt guns, we often surrender to their manipulations and accept total blame for their behavior, pain, or problems.

The strategy of guilt producers is for us to accept responsibility for them and then feel inadequate about ourselves because their lives are such a mess.

Whew! Let's read that again because it describes the process that can occur every time we encounter a difficult person who uses hurt and guilt to manipulate.

People often give in to their guilty feelings and begin telling themselves they are a bad parent, person, employee, child, friend, and the list goes on and on, almost without end if they allow it. The secret to dealing and coping with a difficult person is to choose *not* to allow these manipulations to work and, instead, begin to train or retrain those around us to use and respond to assertive behavior and communication. The difficult person has the power to target us and use their guilt and intimidation tactics, but once we are adults, we *always* have the power to step aside and refuse to accept or reward that behavior.

SOMETIMES I THINK I AM MY OWN WORST ENEMY BECAUSE I AM ALWAYS FEELING BAD OR GUILTY ABOUT SOMETHING I HAVE SAID OR DONE. DO I SIMPLY NEED TO TALK TO MYSELF IN A MORE POSITIVE WAY?

It always amazes me how many people *choose* to stand in place while someone they claim to love, like, or even respect continues to take aim and repeatedly fire at their self-esteem. In fact, many people even *help* the difficult person by taking up the attack themselves with self-judgment and self-criticism. The difficult person may only attack for a few minutes, even seconds, but some people continue to attack themselves for days, months, or years after the actual assault. Sadly enough, we are usually more negative, unforgiving, and critical of ourselves than any other person ever will be. The difficult person relies on us to finish the job. They trust us to be our own worst enemy. In the case of Diane and her mom, Mom often berates herself and her role as a "good" mother long after Diane has the cookie and is off happily playing. Diane planted the seed, but mom kept it growing.

Replaying scenes from the past where we continually question whether we said or did the wrong thing and going over and over what we *should* have done becomes a habit—an addiction that may be difficult to break. If the feelings of guilt, shame, or inadequacy continue for too long, we will soon begin to experience the physical side effects of mental self-abuse: headaches, stomachaches, depression, lack of energy, or many other stress-related illnesses and symptoms.

Stress can often be traced to people or situations that cause you to constantly question yourself in a critical, negative way.

Continual self-criticism and self-doubt is not only stressful, but self-destructive and takes its toll on our physical and emotional well-being.

HOW CAN WE FIGHT THE NEGATIVE FEELINGS GUILT MAY PRODUCE SO WE CAN FEEL OUR BEST BOTH PHYSICALLY AND EMOTIONALLY?

We have several choices, including the following:

1. We can confront the person and assertively deal with the problems, guilt attacks, accusations, insinuations, or threats, and refuse to accept responsibility for them. Then, we can begin to help the person work toward a positive solution (the assertive style).
2. We can *choose* to simply avoid the confrontation at all costs and give in and do what they ask (like Diane's mom when she handed over the cookie [the passive style]).
3. We can become difficult ourselves by crying, whining, yelling, or using various behaviors involving our own manipulations (the aggressive style).
4. We can get even and make them suffer (the passive-aggressive style).

Each response gives some relief, however, only the first choice will have long-term effects that are positive. The second choice, passive, which we will discuss in the next chapter, is a short-term solution that teaches others that we can be manipulated. At the very least, giving in means that we will get to fight the battle for control of our lives every time we encounter the difficult person we have trained. And this is one of the most important points and bears repeating:

We train difficult people!

Too often people opt for the second option—passive. As pointed out in the previous chapter, many of us are neither trained nor experienced in the art of assertive communication, so we often choose simply *not* to deal with issues head on. It feels like a confrontation, and no one likes confrontation. Many of us choose avoidance in difficult situations because it is faster and easier at that moment.

Difficult people are quick to learn from us what we will avoid, accept, and endure. Then, they plan their future encounters with us accordingly.

The third choice (aggressive), becoming difficult ourselves, is tempting, I will admit. It is easy to get caught up in a screaming match, verbal exchange, insults, or criticisms, mutual silent treatment or "who has treated whom the worst" battle.

The problem is that this third option does nothing to make you feel better in the long run, and now the other person either feels superior to you because they invariably calm down and watch you in disgust as you yell or cry, totally out of control, or they may react to your aggressive behavior by feeling equally as guilty as you. "Good," you say, "They deserve it." There is no doubt that it is possible to experience a measure of satisfaction at having inflicted some pain or sadness upon a person who does not hesitate to use it on us. The problem is that nothing has been resolved, the relationship suffers greatly, and the worst result is that *we are now acting exactly the way we are trying to avoid having to deal with in others.*

Then, we have the fourth option (passive-aggressive), payback time: "I'll teach them a lesson." We will learn more about this in an upcoming chapter, but bear in mind that keeping score, paying people back, and teaching them "a lesson" all require great time and energy on our part and do nothing to better the relationship. In fact, you are sure to create an enemy who will now be determined to get even with you.

Do you see how these four communication styles are always available to us? With these four options, we are constantly choosing how to communicate and respond to others in every situation. Sadly, however, many people choose the nonassertive styles far too often.

IT SOUNDS LIKE WE OFTEN OPT FOR THE COMMUNICATION STYLE THAT WORKS THE EASIEST AND QUICKEST RATHER THAN THE ONE THAT WILL HELP US MOST IN THE LONG RUN.

Most definitely! When we start to feel guilt or fear gripping our hearts, we often abandon our rational mind, which tells us to think about the long-term results of our actions. Our conscious, assertive communicator is screaming, "Hang in there! We can deal with this," but instead, we often go for the instant react-and-move-on response. Without a doubt, there is one sure way to make guilt go away quickly: Turn a "no" into a "yes" by doing what they ask, meet their demands, and give up the battle. Mom may think a cookie is a very small price to pay to be rid of those feelings of guilt, sadness, or inadequacy. In fact, how about two cookies? A $5 bill? Are you sure one pair of $100 sneakers is enough? Will a new car make up for all the things I didn't do for you when you were growing up? Or, how about an expensive vacation? And the list goes on and on.

The trouble is, no matter how good it feels at first to give in and get rid of the negative mind and body sensations that accompany guilt and fear, giving in and avoiding the real issues has tragic consequences for our children, employees, family, customers, friends, and *ourselves*. Responding and giving in to manipulation teaches a terrible lesson. People learn that when they make us feel bad, guilty, or insecure, they get what they want—they walk away with the cookie (car, promotion, or paycheck)! Though she may not consciously remember this incident, Diane's subconscious will never forget this lesson. Her subconscious will store it for future reference and whenever she feels thwarted in getting her way, she will be instantly reminded of what behavior worked in the past and will probably use guilt-producing techniques throughout life with her husband, children, and coworkers. And, why not? It has been so effective! I'll repeat again:

We train people to be difficult every
time we reward difficult behavior.

Is this message sinking in? Difficult people cannot survive without us. We play an invaluable role in the dance between us and the difficult person. Without us standing our ground and giving in, their unacceptable behavior would be rendered useless. Once the aggressive is in control, they can usually predict that their opponent will continue to respond the way they want.

Let's now take a look at how anger is as equally effective as hurt when it comes to manipulation. Hurt and anger share the same goal—to get one's needs met through manipulation—and differ only in the delivery. We will work from the same scenario, only our difficult person in training will be an 8-year-old boy, Timmy, with his harried Dad making dinner. Timmy asks for a cookie, but his father tells him, "No, I'm making a good dinner and I don't want you to ruin your appetite. We're having macaroni and cheese."

At this point Timmy's subconscious takes over. Asking respect-fully did *not* work, so let's experiment with some other behaviors. In this case, rather than choose the hurt/guilt ploy, the subconscious urges the little boy to use his temper and pitch a fit (anger). The sce-nario might look like the following:

> Timmy yells, "I hate macaroni and cheese! That's all we ever have around here. I wish Mom was here. She wouldn't care if I had just one cookie. You're just too busy like always. I hate you!"

Now, many of you are thinking, "I would *never* allow a child of mine to talk to me like that." Good for you. It means you have set some boundaries that involve respect and assertive, rather than ag-gressive communication. An assertive parent might respond, "Tim! That is *not* how we talk to one another in this house."

Unfortunately, there are many homes where that is exactly how children talk to their parents *and* walk away with a cookie in their hand (or a scooter, designer jeans, car keys, etc.). Not only do these children fail to learn that aggressive behavior is unacceptable, they are rewarded for their negative outbursts.

Every time a parent fails to model assertive communication their children learn to use manipulation to get their needs met.

Following are some scenarios that you might recognize from situations in your own life:

> Diane (hurt): "I can't believe you don't trust me. You never notice when I clean my room or help around the house because you're too tired. You are stricter than any of my friends' parents. You don't care if I even have a date."

> Timmy (anger): "I can't believe you! You are so old-fashioned. You always work and I have to take care of myself, but when I want to do something, it's a different story. You want to control everything I do. You don't love me!"

I cannot tell you how many teenagers I counseled who admitted they could get almost anything they wanted from their parents by using hurt or anger (or a combination of both).

As adults, Diane and Tim will have become masters at using these manipulative techniques. Listen as Tim and Diane continue to use hurt and anger throughout life to get their needs met.

Diane (using hurt with her spouse who wants to go golfing):
"Sure . . . never mind, go ahead. No, I'll be fine. Someone should have a nice weekend so it might as well be you. Children, don't cry. Maybe next weekend Dad will have time between golf and the football game to spend some time with us [sniff, sniff]." (Goal: make him feel bad or guilty so he will stay home).

Tim (using anger with his spouse who wants to go back to school):
"Great! And what am I supposed to do? Come home after working all day and do your job too—feed the kids and put them to bed? You only think about yourself. No wonder I work long hours. Who would want to come home to this!"

Tim (using anger with his daughter who did not clean her room):
"Look at this. You're just like your mother—always too busy to clean up. You're lazy and totally irresponsible. Why can't you be more like your sister?"

Diane (using hurt when her boss reminds her that a project is overdue):
"You just don't understand. You've given me more work than anyone else and then you put in this new computer system—it's too hard. And, everyone else was late giving me the information I needed. Besides, this has been a really difficult year for me at home [crying now]. I'm trying to do the best I can. You always pick on me lately."

Tim (using anger with boss who wants him to be more punctual):
"What are you doing? Watching me every minute? Lots of people are late, why just point me out? You've never liked me anyway. It used to be different before you came and made all these changes."

IT SOUNDS AS THOUGH ANGER
BORDERS ON VERBAL ABUSE.

Yes, it often does, but we need to understand something about verbal abuse. Verbal abuse rarely has anything to do with the truth. It is about fear, put-downs, and outright attacks on character. People who are using anger to manipulate and as a result become verbally abusive, will say anything that allows them to be in control, even if they must exaggerate or lie. Verbal abuse is full of blame and finger pointing.

A verbally abusive person is desperate to put the responsibility for their actions, failures, and problems on every thing and everyone but themselves.

Verbal abuse sounds like the following:

1. "You're the reason I drink. You've never been there for me."
2. "You want to know why I had an affair? Take a look in the mirror. You don't even care about yourself, let alone me."
3. "All you do is nag. No wonder I don't have a job. You never support me."
4. "You make me scream (hit, yell, etc.). If you'd act the way you should, I wouldn't have to do this."
5. "All you do is nag. No wonder my grades are bad. You don't love me."

These statements are *not true*! People drink excessively, use drugs, refuse to get a job, have affairs, and so forth because of their own issues and insecurities, not because someone else made them do it.

BUT WHY WOULD ANYONE BELIEVE THE LIES AND EXAGGERATIONS, LET ALONE BE INTIMIDATED BY THEM?

The sad answer is that there are many people whose self-esteem and confidence are so low that they will believe what someone else says about them rather than focus on what they know to be true about themselves. The truth is:

Most abuse would not exist without the help of someone who is willing to allow it, accept it, *and* reward it.

Just as humans must have oxygen to survive, abusers of all kinds (physical, mental, emotional, sexual, verbal) must have someone to abuse. Let's clarify one important point: Many abused people are not willing participants! They are truly victims, as in the case of children or victims of crime or war. These people have *no choice* as to how they are treated. They are in a situation over which they have little or no control.

However, many people in abusive situations do have a choice. They are not children and they are not victims, yet they remain planted in place and continue to take shot after shot. If you are reading this book and know right now that you are one of these people— someone who is *choosing* for whatever reason to stay in a relationship that is hurtful, destructive, or even dangerous, then I have only one important piece of advice: get professional help fast!

There are some outstanding books on the market that will assist you in uncovering some important truths about yourself and others, as well as audio and video self-help programs that are effective. But, these are usually supplementary to the professional help you will probably need to support you in making the important, life-affirming changes in self-esteem, behavior, and attitude necessary to get your life back on a solid and emotionally healthy foundation. Think for a moment: If you are afraid to leave this person or situation, just imagine what *might* and probably *will* happen if you continue to stay in the relationship.

If, however, you are not in a potentially destructive or dangerous situation, but rather find yourself constantly in situations with difficult but nonviolent people, then books, workshops, and tape programs may definitely help change your life.

CAN I BE ASSERTIVE AND STILL GET ANGRY?

Of course. Anger is not always manipulative. In fact, releasing pent-up anger can often be downright therapeutic and even necessary to our well-being. Just as there are meaningful and appropriate times to be hurt, there are also situations where anger is justified. Assertive anger, however, is different from manipulative anger. Assertive anger expresses an emotion, but the goal is not to frighten, belittle, abuse, or destroy the other person or their self-esteem. Assertive anger is communicated as a means to move into problem solving. For example, "I'm very angry about what happened, and I don't want it to happen again. Let's talk about what we need to do to fix the problem so we can move on." Notice that there are no threats, no put-downs, no attacks on the person's character—just an honest expression of a person's feelings with resolution being the goal in an attempt to create a win/win situation and maintain a healthy relationship with the other person. Assertive anger is by no means to be taken lightly, but it is backed up by fairness, integrity, consistency, and forthrightness rather than fear, threats, put-downs, or force.

People often misunderstand assertive communication and think they cannot express their sad or angry feelings and must stay in perfect control of their emotions at all times. No way! Assertive people feel hurt, sad, and betrayed and can effectively use the assertive style to express these feelings so that others can empathize, sympathize, and offer needed support. Also, people can feel angry and use the assertive style to convey that emotion. In fact, as we will discuss in the next chapter, the problem with passive people is that they do *not* express their anger effectively; therefore, we never know where we stand or how they truly feel about a situation. The important difference is when someone is expressing assertive anger, you do not feel afraid or threatened because you are not being personally attacked. In fact, their anger does not usually even involve you. It may be about getting cut off in traffic, an unfair situation at work, or bad weather spoiling a great day.

Manipulative anger, on the other hand, is not so mature, wise, or rational. Manipulative anger is generally unfair, hostile, and threatening, and often renders the unassertive opponent incapable of responding, which is exactly what the difficult person is hoping for.

SOMETIMES I HAVE A DIFFICULT TIME DIFFERENTIATING BETWEEN ASSERTIVE ANGER AND AGGRESSIVE ANGER. IS THERE AN EASY WAY FOR ME TO TELL WHICH ONE SOMEONE IS USING?

Well, one way is to listen to the noun they use to begin their sentences. Assertive anger almost always begins sentences with the word, *I,* because there is no desire to attack or place blame. When we begin with *I,* we are usually accepting responsibility for our choices and feelings, such as the following:

1. *"I* asked you to have the kitchen cleaned by dinner. It's not done. *I* need you to accept responsibility for your jobs around the house and do them without being reminded. *I* feel angry when I have to remind you to do your share."

2. *"I* know you work hard and want some time alone on the weekends to play golf, but *I* have the same need and I'm angry that I never have quality time alone to do the things I enjoy. *I* need to work out a compromise with you so that each of us has some time to ourselves."

3. *"I* know that you are having some problems in your personal life right now, but *I'm* angry that you spend so much work time making personal phone calls. *I'm* having to pick up your extra work as a result, and I don't think that's fair."

Assertive anger states the problem *and* the possible solution without attacking the other person's character or dignity.

Aggressive anger is very different. Notice that the first word out of an aggressive's mouth is usually *you*, not *I*. The word *you* usually precedes an attack, complaint or criticism, as in the following examples:

1. "Look at this kitchen! *You* never listen to me. *You* never just pitch in and help without me having to nag you. *You* have eyes in your head. *You* can see what needs to be done! Am I your maid?!"

2. "All *you* do is play golf! *You* don't care about me or the kids. *You* do whatever you want when you want it. *You* are totally selfish and self-centered."

3. "If *you* think I'm going to keep covering for *you* because you have personal problems, then *you* are wrong. *You* can never handle anything. Why don't *you* just leave him and go on with your life? *You* always make stupid choices and then expect the rest of us to pick up the pieces!"

See a difference? Assertive anger leaves a person with their self-respect intact. It does not use control, put-downs, or power plays, but focuses on compromise and negotiation so the problem can be solved and the relationship can move ahead. Aggressive anger wants to elicit change not by negotiation, but through intimidation, threats, and put-downs. Aggressives are on the path to power and control. Assertives are on the path to a solution.

IS IT AS EASY TO TELL THE DIFFERENCE BETWEEN ASSERTIVE HURT AND AGGRESSIVE HURT?

Yes. In fact, look for the same two clue words: *I* and *you*. Look at the differences in the following scenarios.

"*I* feel badly that we haven't been getting along lately. *I* remember how we used to talk and help each other. *I* know I haven't been as caring about you and your needs lately as I want to be. Perhaps you are feeling the same. *I'd* like to change the way things are."

Whereas aggressive hurt might sound more like the following:

"*You* obviously don't love me anymore. *You* never talk to me or do nice things. *You* don't even seem to want to be with me. *You* like your job better than me. *You* don't know how much *you* hurt me."

Even though the *I* and *you* test often works when listening for signs to determine which communication style the other person is using, difficult people can be tricky. I remember a woman who attended one of my group sessions on assertiveness. I had worked with her to understand her tendency to manipulate and control everyone around her. She returned to the group the next week following our session on using the assertive *I* and avoiding the aggressive *you*, very proud to announce that she had tried the new technique. We all congratulated her and asked her to repeat what happened. She said, "Well, I approached one of my employees who had come in tardy and told her, '*I* think you are irresponsible. *I'm* tired of you never thinking about anyone other than yourself, and *I* suggest you decide whether you want to keep this job!' " Can you see a disturbing pattern? It is true that her sentences began with the word *I*, but they were definitely messages based on the second noun, *you*.

DOES IT CHANGE HOW PEOPLE RESPOND TO US WHEN WE BEGIN OUR SENTENCES WITH THE WORD *YOU?*

Oh, yes! We are usually going to do one of two things when we begin a sentence with the word *you*. We will either praise and compliment the other person or attack, put-down, criticize, and tell them what to do. Therefore, when we hear the word *you*, we generally steel ourselves for an attack because *you* is used far more often to impart a negative message than a positive one. In the preceding scenarios, the word *you* was always followed by an attack. What does the average person do when they are attacked? They defend themselves. Following are some examples of how someone might defend themselves after a *you* attack:

1. "I am *not* a bad husband (mother, daughter, friend, etc.)."

2. "I *do* love you. I've just been busy."

3. "I don't *always* make personal calls on work time. Usually I make them on my break."

And when we are done defending ourselves, what usually happens? We then go on the attack! Such as the following:

1. "*You* should talk! *You* spend half the day talking about your new boyfriend."

2. "I didn't clean the kitchen because *you* didn't go to the store and buy new supplies. In fact, *you* never go to the store at all anymore. *You* care more about your job than you do about me."

3. "Free time? All I want is 2 hours a weekend to myself. *You* made me feel like I can never to anything I want unless I'm with you and the kids. *You* have no clue how hard I work. *You* never understand!"

One of the most common fights in a marriage, family, or workplace is the *you-I-you* fight. One person attacks, the other defends and then attacks back. (Who has the toughest day, hardest job, most stressful commute, etc.) Assertiveness is forgotten in the pursuit of who can outdo the other in the areas of criticism, threats, and put-downs.

Assertive anger and assertive hurt allow the relationship to grow in a healthy way. It is hard to feel good about someone or love someone when you are constantly being attacked and attacking back. When I was counseling couples who were trying to work on their marriage, the first three traits I looked for to determine whether they were communicating aggressively were: criticsm, contempt (sarcasm, ridicule, etc.), and defensiveness. These three traits indicated to me that nonassertive communication was being used most often, and the confidence and trust needed to build the relationship had been damaged or even destroyed. An unhealthy pattern had been established: Someone criticized, the other defended, and then either gave in (and felt resentful) or criticized back.

On the other hand, what a wonderful word *you* becomes when it begins a well-deserved or much needed compliment, such as in the following statements:

1. *"You* are so dear to me. *You* make me feel loved and special."
2. *"You* are such a big help. Look at this house! *You* did a great job, and I didn't even have to remind you."
3. *"You* really are a valuable employee. *You* take charge and are always so professional. Thank you for your support."

These are great examples of the assertive *you* at work.

IT IS EASY TO SEE HOW THE BEHAVIORS WE LEARNED AS CHILDREN MAY DETERMINE HOW WE GET OUR NEEDS MET AS WE GROW OLDER.

Yes. Do not forget that difficult people have had years of experience mastering their act. And, that is exactly what it is: an act! My sister Vicki and I are both speakers and authors, but we are also actors. We can act sad and hurt, or angry and threatening at a moment's notice, depending on the part we must play. Difficult people are also actors. They can act hurt or angry depending on what works to get their needs met. Therefore, to successfully deal with these manipulative behaviors you must first view difficult people as actors who use gimmicks, role-playing, and theatrics to play their part in life, which is all about getting what they want (often at your expense).

Once you identify them as masterful actors rather than scary, hurtful, or intimidating people, then you can begin to resist the temptation to take their comments personally. Remember, as in the case of verbal abuse, many things the difficult person says are not even true (or at least they are seriously exaggerated).

DO MEN AND WOMEN USE DIFFERENT TECHNIQUES WHEN THEY ARE USING MANIPULATION?

I am sure you have noticed that the examples given so far that used hurt and guilt to get one's needs met usually involved women, and the examples using anger usually involved men. It has been my experience that women tend to use the hurt strategy more often than men. Men, on the other hand, tend to use anger more often as their manipulative tool of choice.

Women may resort to hurt feelings and guilt more often than men because as young girls we were more likely to be rewarded and fussed over when we were sad and hurt, whereas little boys were not. Boys generally were told to stop crying, whereas little girls received positive attention (i.e., acting hurt was rewarded). Expressing hurt feelings is not perceived as being as aggressive as expressing anger, so it was more acceptable for girls to react in this manner. Men, on the other hand, are often more comfortable than women with loud voices, yelling to be heard, and other more overtly aggressive forms of communication. Anger in small boys is often viewed as simply "boys will be boys," but not tolerated as lady-like in little girls.

Interestingly enough, however, this creates a perfect (but unhealthy) match in the world of imperfect relationships because women tend to give in more when confronted by anger, and men often cave in when surrounded by tears, sadness, and hurt. Some men may feel a need to care for and protect people, and this may make them more easily coerced by people who use hurt to get their way, whereas some women may try to placate anger and thus give in more readily to that technique.

However, let there be no mistake. In therapy sessions, I worked with plenty of angry, even abusive, women and sad, guilt-producing men. So, stereotypes are just that—generalizations. As much as I want to avoid stereotyping, however, it is still very apparent that men and women often have some deep-seated communication patterns that they have a tendency to fall into. However, the more both sexes understand those traps, the sooner we can work to avoid them. Each sex appears to be trying to change these patterns. Professional women understand that hurt feelings and tears have no place at work, and men are learning that anger does not garner respect. Unfortunately, working together has allowed some difficult people of both sexes the opportunity to simply expand their arsenal of manipulative weapons rather than eliminate them altogether in favor of assertive behavior. Unfortunately, Vicki and I are discovering that many difficult people have become masters at using both hurt and anger. If one is not successful, they simply try the other.

The good news is that we can all change how we deal with and react to these negative behaviors.

Summary

- The two emotions used most frequently to manipulate others are *hurt* and *anger.*
- We are responsible *to* people, not *for* people.
- When difficult people use hurt to manipulate, their goal is to make us feel guilty or bad about ourselves.
- When people use anger to manipulate, their goal is to frighten or intimidate us.
- When we reward negative and manipulative behavior, that behavior will occur again.
- Difficult people are in a war for control, and they will go to any length to win.
- Guilt is one of the most debilitating emotions we can feel because it causes us to doubt ourselves and thus feel unworthy and inadequate.
- Stress can often be traced to people or situations that cause you to constantly question yourself in a critical, negative way.
- Every time a parent fails to model assertive communication, their children learn to use manipulation to get their needs met.
- Most abuse would not exist without the help of someone who is willing to allow it, accept it, *and* even reward the abuse by giving in.
- Anger can often turn into verbal abuse.
- A verbally abusive person is desperate to put the responsibility for their actions, failures, and problems on everything and everyone except themselves.
- Assertive communication almost always begins with the word *I* because there is no desire to attack or blame others.
- Assertive anger states the problem *and* the possible solution without attacking the other person's character or dignity.
- Aggressive anger almost always begins with the word *you* because there is a desire to attack and blame others.

Take Action

- Identify three situations where someone used hurt to get what they wanted. Were they rewarded for their manipulative behavior? Using assertive communication, how could you resolve the situation?

- Identify three situations where someone used anger to get what they wanted. Were they rewarded for their manipulative behavior? Using assertive communication, how could you resolve the situation?

- Look at your communication style this week. Identify the times you are tempted to use hurt or anger to manipulate someone. How could you be more assertive instead?

5

DEALING WITH THE AGGRESSIVE PERSON

Let's briefly review the preceding chapter. The aggressive personality views life from a win/lose perspective, and they create oppositional relationships. Interactions with them become struggles for control of our personality and our life. Their weapons of choice are hurt and anger, their strategy is to make you feel bad, and their outcome is for you to change your mind, your attitude, or your behavior.

NOW THAT I UNDERSTAND WHY AND HOW AGGRESSIVE PEOPLE MANIPULATE, WHAT CAN I DO TO CHANGE THEM?

This is a good place to reemphasize one important point discussed in Chapter 1:

We cannot change anyone else. We can only change ourselves and how we react to others' attempts to manipulate us.

As long as the difficult person is allowed to behave in an inappropriate or unacceptable way, and as long as they are rewarded for this same behavior by getting their needs met, they will have absolutely *no* incentive to change and become the nice, assertive people we would like them to be. We must change how we react to and communicate with the difficult person.

78

amazon.com

Billing Address:

Regina Kapose
1708 Second Ave 55
New York, NY 10128
United States

Shipping Address:

Regina Kapose
9710-1011A Mariposa #4119
LaCanda Wen O5, CA 9263-4146
United States

SD6Y75XpRR

Returns Are Easy!

Visit http://www.amazon.com/returns to return any item to us including gifts, in unopened or original condition within 30 days for a full refund (other restrictions apply)

Your order of August 25, 2009 (Order ID: 102 3751777 - 9160(245)

Qty.	Item	Item Price	Total
1	**Life Would Be Easy if It Weren't for Other People** ("P-4-1438") 0803968635 0803968635 0803968635 Paperback	$26.05	$26.05

Subtotal		$26.05
Shipping & Handling		$1.99
Promotional Certificate		$1.99
Shipment Total		$26.05
Paid via Visa		$26.05
Balance Due		$0.00

We've sent this part of your order to ensure quicker service. The other items will ship separately at no additional shipping cost

Have feedback on how we packaged your order? Tell us at www.amazon.com/packaging

(1 of 1)

SD6Y75XpRR

9/D6Y75XpRR/-1 of 1 //1Mecon-us/5015719/0831-23:00/0827:22:54 V3

amazon.com
and you're done.

WHAT OPTIONS DO I HAVE WHEN I AM CONFRONTED WITH A DIFFICULT, AGGRESSIVE PERSON?

When faced with aggressive behavior, we have two possible responses. First, we can assert ourselves, confront the attack (which means we avoid reacting to the emotions and sensations their tactics trigger in us), and neutralize the onslaught. This is the assertive choice. Second, we can allow ourselves to be drawn in and manipulated and respond by using one of the three nonassertive communication styles. We can give in to the attack and avoid the issue at hand (passive), we can resort to imitating the difficult behavior by being manipulative right back (aggressive), or we can attempt to get even and teach them a lesson (passive-aggressive). Remember, every time we give in to aggressive behavior, difficult people learn that we are susceptible to their manipulations, and they are storing information on how they will treat us in the future. I doubt you need any instruction in how to implement the second response: All you need to do is give in, give out, or give up. However, if you are like most people, you may need help implementing the first strategy: assertively dealing with a nonassertive person.

WHY IS IT SO HARD FOR MANY OF US TO BE ASSERTIVE AND CONFRONT THE DIFFICULT PERSON?

There are three main reasons:

First, as we discussed before, many people have never learned how to be assertive; therefore, past experiences with difficult people have proven to be frustrating, nonproductive, and even traumatic. With that record, who wouldn't avoid future confrontation? These people need to understand *how* and *why* difficult people act and say what they do and then learn the communication skills necessary to deal with difficult people.

Second, many people have not been making good, ethical, healthy choices and, therefore, their self-esteem is low. Without self-confidence, it is not easy to stand up for oneself and deal maturely and assertively with the difficult person. These people need to slowly begin making better choices—one at a time—about themselves and their relationships so they can begin to develop their self-esteem. Their first step should be to commit to the belief that each person has a right to be treated respectfully.

The third reason may be the most important of all three. Most of us want to be nice people, and we may view assertiveness as too confrontational and not at all fitting our perception of nice behavior. Often, we think it would be better to avoid the confrontation and hope their behavior does not continue. Unfortunately, not only will their behavior continue, but it will probably worsen, and we have now become an integral part of the problem.

WHY WOULD THE DIFFICULT PERSON GET WORSE IF WE AVOID THE ISSUE AND TRY TO MOVE ON?

The bottom line is:

Difficult people do not respect people who lack the courage and self-respect to stand up to them and their manipulative behavior.

The irony of the situation is that difficult people want their own way and desperately want to be in control, but at the same time, they do not respect the people who fall for and give in to their manipulations. They grudgingly withhold their admiration for those people who either do not fall for their antics and manipulations or those who can dish it back.

It is as though deep down the difficult person realizes how inappropriately they treat others and are waiting to see just how far they can go with their whining, crying, screaming, and threats without being held accountable. Remember, when we discussed boundaries we stated that difficult people are masters at detecting what your limits are and instantly know how much they can get away with in terms of what you will accept and even reward. Take a look around and notice for a moment—every difficult person does treat a few people better than others. They rarely play out their act on those individuals. Usually, those people are very assertive, confident, and comfortable with themselves, and this seems to put the difficult person on their best (or better) behavior. We have just discovered an important truth:

Most difficult people are cowards!

They really do not want to deal with anyone they think might see through the tears and threats and assertively take them on face-to-face.

I remember watching a television documentary about bears where they stated that if you were to run into a bear, the best thing to do is stand still, look the bear in the eyes and let it know you are not afraid (probably easier said than done). If you can do this, there is a chance the bear will back away and not attack. Well, the same advice holds true for difficult people—stand still (and, I think it should be far easier to stand your ground in the face of a difficult person than in the presence of a bear!). As soon as they know you feel afraid, inadequate, confused, inferior, or guilty, they will attack. The difficult person feeds off of our fearful, tearful responses and reactions.

DO I REALLY CARE WHETHER THE DIFFICULT PERSON RESPECTS ME?

First of all, assertive communication allows you to respect yourself because you are insisting on fair, ethical treatment. Second, when the difficult person begins to respect you, their need and desire to play games with you will be lessened considerably. Some difficult people can be quite polite, cooperative, and accommodating in relationships with people they respect. Many people, however, try to achieve respect by being nonassertive and avoiding the aggressive person or ignoring their inappropriate behavior. It does not work that way. Hoping people will like you because you ignore their unacceptable behavior does not create respect from the difficult person or from yourself. In fact, it simply increases the odds that they will continue to treat you badly.

WHEN I THINK OF CONFRONTATION, I THINK OF FIGHTING, ARGUING, HOSTILITY, AND ANGER. WHY SHOULDN'T I AVOID THESE THINGS?

Perhaps one of the main reasons why people avoid assertive communication, especially if it involves some element of confrontation, is because they view any form of negative feedback as argumentative, hostile, or critical. The aggressive person has already set the tone for a potentially stressful situation, so the feeling generally is, "Why make it worse by saying how I really feel. They are angry (or hurt) already." Well, that part is true enough. They are already angry and/or hurt, and it is usually quite effective. They are now counting on you to do exactly what you usually do—let it go, ignore them, and give in to their demands.

In Chapter 1, we learned that there are three kinds of feedback:

1. Positive
2. Negative
3. Ignore/avoid

When we give someone positive feedback (a reward), the likelihood is that the action or behavior will be repeated. When we give someone negative feedback, it becomes more complicated. First of all, there are two distinct categories of negative feedback. Unfortunately, the one most of us think about first when we hear the term *negative feedback*, usually involves some form of anger, put-downs, sarcasm, threats, yelling, punishment, or pain. I refer to this as *aggressive negative*.

Examples may include the following:

1. "You are so lazy and irresponsible. How many times do I have to tell you to clean up your room?" (put-downs)
2. "You don't love me. You never pay attention to me." (anger, accusations)
3. "Oh fine. That's a great idea. I'm sure our clients will really enjoy waiting 2 extra days for their order." (sarcasm)
4. "I'm sick of dealing with you! I've had it!" (yelling)
5. "You want to fight me on this—fine, but just try to get that promotion you want." (threats)

These are just a few of the many statements we repeatedly hear in every day life that represents how most negative feedback sounds. No wonder most of us would like to avoid being like that.

The secret to assertive communication is the second category of negative feedback: It is what I refer to as *assertive negative*. Assertive negative allows us to give negative feedback concerning someone's actions, attitudes, or behaviors in a positive, assertive, and productive way without damaging the person or their self-esteem.

HOW CAN ANY NEGATIVE FEEDBACK BE NICE?

It is *nice* to be honest. It is *nice* to let someone know where they stand with you. It also is *nice* to set fair limits and expectations so people can grow. On the other hand, I see nothing nice about allowing someone to continue believing that their angry or hurtful behavior is acceptable to you. I also see nothing nice about allowing yourself to be mistreated or disrespected. The only way any of us learn to act, talk, and treat others respectfully is by being in the presence of people assertive, caring, and courageous enough to model how decent, cooperative, professional people behave and communicate. This process must include both praise and positive feedback for things we have done well and assertive, negative feedback when we are out of line.

People who always worry about being "nice at all costs" usually have a problem giving any negative feedback. As a result, they do a serious disservice to those who look to them for lessons on how to form successful, healthy relationships. When we engage in assertive negative, we are allowing someone to know that their behavior is not acceptable or appropriate. But, we do it in a way that shows respect for the person and the relationship. Aggressive negative uses threats, abuse, yelling, and put-downs and will only get in the way of the other person hearing us. They will respond to the tone and the attacks rather than the message. They will become defensive, move into aggressive communication and begin to react using either hurt or anger just as they witnessed you doing to them. Now, your worst fears are confirmed: You will have escalated the situation into a battle, which can be hostile and argumentative—just what you were trying to avoid.

The scenario often goes like this: We try be nice and not make waves. The situation becomes so intolerable that we finally lose control of our emotions and become aggressive. We either cry and fall apart saying, "I don't deserve this," or we become angry and go on the attack yelling, "You are selfish and irresponsible. I hate you!" Either choice makes the situation worse. The difficult person, realizing we can be manipulated, moves in for the kill. Nothing is solved and the situation is worse than ever. Now, the nice person feels badly and decides it is all their fault because they spoke up. They figure it is just easier to say nothing the next time. The problem is that neither party used the assertive style of communication. First, we were passive and avoided the issue, then we became aggressive and used manipulation. Finally, we felt badly and decided to be passive again.

Assertive negative means you *must* let the other person know as soon as possible that their action, tone, or behavior is *not* acceptable to you, *if* you do not want the behavior to occur again. If you give in, it will happen again. If you ignore it, it will happen again. If you threaten, yell, abuse, or become sarcastic, you will initiate a power struggle, and they will either come back at you even stronger or go underground (passive-aggressive, which we will discuss in the next chapter) and get you behind your back. The *only* communication style that will have a chance of eliminating or dealing with aggressive behavior is assertive, which involves the ability to use assertive negative whenever necessary.

WHAT DOES "ASSERTIVE NEGATIVE" SOUND LIKE?

Assertive negative sounds mature and grown-up. It sounds functional and healthy. It sounds professional. It sounds in-control and confident. It can even sound caring and comforting. Think about it: Isn't it comforting in today's world of scams, gimmicks, and office politics to be with someone you trust enough to tell you how they feel and where you stand in a confident, respectful way? How great it would be if everyone could or would do that for us.

Let's take those same aggressive negative examples listed earlier on page 83 and turn them into assertive negative statements.

1. "Son, I need you to clean your room *now*. I know you've had a lot going on after school, and it's easy to get distracted, but this needs to be your No. 1 priority."

2. "I've missed you. I enjoy being with you, but I think we've both become so busy at work that we've forgotten to take time to be together. How can we work on this?"

3. "I'm concerned that the new shipping schedule will cause a delay in getting our clients their orders on time. What can we do to make sure this doesn't happen?"

4. "I'm frustrated and tired right now, and I'm sure you are too, so we're getting nowhere with this discussion. Let's talk again later."

5. "We need your support to make this work. This new project represents the vision and mission of our company. As a potential leader of our organization, please think about whether you agree with the direction we're headed. It will be confusing to our employees if we aren't a team."

As you read each example of assertive negative, notice that three important things occur:

1. The other person has been told (or given warning) that we have noticed their behavior, *and* we feel it is not acceptable, appropriate, or necessary.

2. There were no insults, put-downs, sarcastic statements, or threats used when giving the feedback.

3. We did not ignore, reward, accept, or emulate their negative behavior.

BUT, WHAT IF THE OTHER PERSON DOES NOT STOP THEIR NEGATIVE BEHAVIOR? WHAT IF THEY JUST EXPLAIN OR DEFEND WHAT THEY DID? WON'T THIS ESCALATE INTO AN ARGUMENT?

Interestingly enough, the difficult person rarely defends, apologizes for, or excuses *anything* they do. They have had a lifetime of convincing themselves that they are right and justified in acting the way they do. In fact, think back for a moment: It is usually the other way around. *We* often begin to deny, defend, excuse, and even apologize for *our* behavior as though we were wrong. This is one of the reasons why many of us absolutely hate dealing with the difficult person and why we will often go to great lengths to avoid them. It is not pleasant or comfortable to constantly be on the defensive.

HOW DO WE COMMUNICATE ASSERTIVELY WITH A DIFFICULT PERSON WITHOUT RESORTING TO DEFENSIVENESS, ARGUMENTS, OR APOLOGIES?

Earlier in the book, I gave an analogy of driving a car toward a specific destination and having a passenger who wants to constantly take us off course on detours. Well, let's take that a step further. Think of the difficult person as someone who is detouring our thoughts, our beliefs, even our actions, away from what we know we should do or say. They are purposely trying to get us off the subject so that they can control the discussion and follow their own agenda. Every time we take those detours, we become more and more lost until we finally just give up and let them take the wheel. We give up our control every time we take their detours. Look for all the detours in the following scenario with Alex, the manager, and Roger, the employee. Ask yourself an important question, "Who is in charge of this discussion?"

Alex: "Roger, I need to talk to you about your tardiness. Work starts at 8 a.m., and today you came in at 8:20 a.m. I need you to be on time."

Roger: "I can't believe it. Everyone is late once in a while, and I don't see you talking to them. What about Nancy? She's never on time." (detour)

Alex: "Well, I don't think Nancy has anything to do with you. Nancy has had some personal problems, and she and I have discussed her timeliness before." (Alex took the detour and is now on the defense)

Roger: "Besides, you're always picking on me. Nothing I do is ever right with you." (detour)

Alex (taking the detour): "That's not true. I'm very pleased with the work you're doing." (Smart Roger now has Alex complimenting him about his work.)

Roger: "And you never notice all the times I stay late—long after everyone else has left. I think a lot of people take advantage of me." (detour)

Alex (hopping off on another detour): "Well, Roger, I'm sorry you feel that way. [Now Roger has Alex apologizing.] Just try to be on time from now on."

Try to be on time! It seems unbelievable that Roger has his boss literally begging him to try to be on time, but that is what difficult people do so masterfully. They turn the tables and before we know it, *we* are the ones backing off, defending, and apologizing. Was there any doubt as to who was in charge of this conversation? Alex, the manager, should have been in charge, but Roger led the discussion from the very beginning.

Let's look at another scenario between a mom and her daughter. Can you identify the detours?

Mom: "Jenny, your curfew is midnight. Last Saturday you were late. I need you to be on time tonight."

Jenny (initiating the first detour): "But Mom, that's ridiculous. I'm 17! Don't you trust me? What could I do after midnight that I couldn't do before?"

Mom (jumping right off the subject of curfew and onto the detour): "But Jenny, I do trust you. It's not a matter of trust."

Jenny: "Besides, everyone else can stay out later. Nobody else's parents are as strict as you." (going for an age-old detour)

Mom: "Well, if everyone else jumped off the bridge, would you? This isn't about everyone else." (Mom is now defensive and using old clichés she heard her mom use.)

Jenny: "Never mind. I won't even go to the party. I feel so stupid when I always have to be the first one to leave." (threats—another detour)

Mom: "Well, maybe we can make it a little later. I don't want you to miss the party."

Who is in charge? Who manipulated and who got rewarded? Is it any wonder we have so many difficult people in all walks of life? They manipulate us, and we let them get away with it.

HOW CAN I STOP TAKING THE DETOURS AND STAY FOCUSED ON MY MESSAGE?

First, learn to be observant and begin to recognize all the detours presented to you in everyday conversation. People detour at work, at home, in church, on the golf course—you name it! How do you stay on track? Be aware of detours and refuse to take them. Think about what you need to say, how you want to say it, and stick to the subject—your subject, not theirs. Remember, assertiveness requires us to think about what we are going to say rather than just reacting. When someone tries to detour you, simply repeat your needs over again without responding to the detour.

Alex: "Roger, I need you to be at work, on time, at 8 a.m."

Roger: "But . . . " (detour)

Alex: "I understand, but I need you here on time."

You do not need to make excuses, defend yourself, or apologize. Just state your needs firmly and repeat, if necessary. If you do not get their attention, then you may need to add a consequence and let them know assertively what will happen if the behavior does not change.

Alex (manager): "Roger, I need to let you know that this is your first verbal warning about being late to work. If it happens again, I will issue a written warning."

Mom: "Jenny, I'm not repeating myself again. Your curfew is midnight. If you choose not to accept the responsibility to be on time, then you will not be able to go out with your friends at all next weekend."

You just witnessed assertive negative at work. Although letting someone know what the consequences are is not always easy, it is a necessary part of healthy relationships.

DOES THIS TECHNIQUE ALWAYS WORK? IF WE STAY ON TRACK AND AVOID DETOURS, WILL DIFFICULT PEOPLE RESPOND DIFFERENTLY RIGHT AWAY?

No way! Did you really think it would be that easy? Difficult people are not fools, and they have had a lifetime of success playing their games. They may be momentarily stunned because they seldom run into anyone who is willing or able to stand up to them, but they will not be ready to give up this quickly. Remember, earlier I stated that it often gets worse before it gets better. They may go on the offensive, dig in, no holds barred, and use every trick in the book. The difficult person usually moves into hurt or anger with great intensity—either cries, moans, and complains harder or yells, screams, and threatens louder.

THEN WHAT HAVE I ACCOMPLISHED? HAVEN'T I STILL CREATED MORE STRESS?

For the moment, yes. But, two important things are happening in the relationship.

1. *You know you have not lost control.* You also know you have not allowed yourself to be mistreated or manipulated. You have made a good, healthy choice to be assertive, and you have neither given in nor resorted to using their aggressive tactics, which means your self-esteem level is on an upward swing. You have a little more confidence in your tone and demeanor. You have made it through level one, and you are still intact.

2. *The difficult person will pick up on your level of confidence.* A glimmer of respect is beginning to form. Remember, difficult people have

no respect for the people who allow them to get away with their manipulative antics. Even though they will escalate their behavior, it is done with a little less swagger and a little more begrudging admiration for your "cool." Never forget that assertiveness is very comforting to be around, even for the difficult person.

WHAT DO I DO WHEN THE DIFFICULT PERSON'S BEHAVIOR GETS WORSE?

Stand your ground. Face the bear and deliver your message again. This is the true test. Will assertive or aggressive behavior win out? Often this is where even the most confident person begins to apologize.

> **Alex:** "Roger, *I'm sorry*, but if you continue to be late, I have no choice but to write you a verbal warning."
>
> **Mom:** "Jenny, *I'm sorry*, but I believe that midnight is a fair curfew."

Why are Mom and Alex apologizing? Why do any of us say "we're sorry" when we are only asking for what is right and fair? You might recognize some of these examples:

> "John, *I'm sorry*, but I need you to watch the kids while I go to the store."
>
> "Jessica, *I'm sorry*, but I need you to clean your room before dinner."
>
> "*I'm sorry*, but that's just the way it is."

Let's make a very important point about apologies. The three words, "I am sorry," can be three of the strongest words in the English language or three of the weakest words. An apology should only be given when one of the following two things are true:

1. A serious mistake was made.
2. The intent is for it never to happen again.

Look back and reread the apologies. Did Alex make a serious mistake by asking Roger to come to work on time? Does he intend to never again ask him to be punctual? Did Mom make a serious error in asking Jenny to be home by midnight? Does she intend to never enforce a curfew again? Obviously not; therefore, the words, *I'm sorry*, are weak and play right into the difficult person's hands.

WHEN WILL THE DIFFICULT PERSON GET BETTER? HOW LONG WILL IT TAKE?

The honest truth is that they may never get better. Then you have a very important decision to make. You must first admit to yourself that this person and situation may *never* improve no matter how assertive you become. You have used every assertive technique possible and they will not budge.

You are left with the following two options:

1. Stay in the relationship, *accept* that this is the way it is, and stop complaining, or
2. Sever the relationship because the situation is unacceptable.

WHY TRY TO BE ASSERTIVE WHEN IT MAY NOT EVEN WORK?

For several reasons, including the following:

1. Assertiveness usually *does* work, and when it does, the results are wonderful—a chance to live or work with someone without the stress and tension you experienced before.
2. No matter what, *you* will respect yourself better if you behave and communicate without manipulation. You will feel no shame or guilt because you know you did not resort to aggressive behavior and instead dealt with the situation in a mature, healthy way.
3. If assertiveness does not work, then you can make the necessary choice to get out of the relationship and move on to a healthier place in life without wondering whether you were to blame or could have done more to salvage the relationship. You know you did your best, but it is senseless to continue to waste your time and energy on a potentially destructive situation.

4. If you care about the difficult person at all, you owe them the opportunity to learn from you how to incorporate respect and assertiveness into their communication patterns.

5. Assertiveness is the *only* functional and healthy way to communicate and behave. You really have no choice if you want what is best for yourself and the people you love.

6. If you have children, you owe it to them to model the healthiest and most functional behavior so they can learn from your assertive example.

SHOULD WE NEVER EXPLAIN OURSELVES OR GIVE A REASON FOR OUR ACTIONS?

Of course people deserve a reason and an explanation. I have assumed that this was done in the beginning. Assertive people let people know up front what is expected and they encourage others to participate in setting those expectations.

An assertive employer would have explained to Roger from the first day what the time schedule was. An assertive parent would have had a discussion with the teenager *before* they even got their driver's license and talked about limits, curfews, and rules regarding where to drive, who is in the car, and so forth.

With rational, assertive people, you can take a detour now and then and be safe. You can give a reason, re-explain a direction, and so on, but this book is not about our conversations with functional, rational, assertive human beings. This book is about dealing with difficult, often irrational human beings who require, demand, and play by different rules.

The communication technique that uses repetition while avoiding detours works! It allows us to stay in charge, not lose control, gives assertive negatives without resorting to avoidance or manipulation, and maintains our dignity and self-respect. What more can we ask for from any conversation?

The best way to communicate with a difficult person is stating your needs without attacking, resisting their attempts to detour you away from the subject, avoiding defensiveness, excuses, apologies (unless warranted), and standing firm. Recognize that this may or may not work. If it works, then you have moved the relationship into a healthier territory. If it does not work, then you at least know where you stand, and you can *choose* to either stay or leave the relationship. Sound easy? No way. Becoming assertive is not a simple solution, but it is the *only* solution if you want your relationship to be successful, healthy, and happy.

WHAT IF I STILL CHOOSE TO JUST IGNORE DIFFICULT PEOPLE AND PUT UP WITH THEM AS BEST AS I CAN BY DOING WHATEVER I HAVE TO DO TO KEEP THEM AS HAPPY AS POSSIBLE? WHAT COMMUNICATION STYLE IS THAT, AND WILL IT WORK?

It sounds as though you have decided to be passive, a communication style many people choose to use over and over again in their lives when dealing with difficult people. Will it work? Well, it is going to take a whole chapter to answer that, so let's move ahead and discuss our third communication style: passive.

Summary

- We cannot change anyone else. We can only change ourselves and how we react to others' attempts to manipulate us.

- As long as a difficult person is allowed to behave in an inappropriate or unacceptable way, and they are rewarded for this behavior by getting their needs met, they will have *no* incentive to change.

- Most difficult people are cowards.

- Aggressive people want control. They want to get their needs met and have been taught (by the rest of us) that manipulation using hurt and anger usually works.

- Many people try to avoid confrontation because they believe a confrontation will simply escalate the already tense situation, or they believe any type of confrontation or negative feedback will not coincide with their image of a "nice" person.

- Difficult people do not respect people who allow them to get away with their manipulations; therefore, we must give the difficult person timely feedback (assertive negative) that their behavior is not acceptable.

Take Action

- Think of a situation where someone has tried to detour you away from the subject.

    Did their technique work?

    Will it work next time?

- Think of an aggressive person in your life who uses hurt to get their way.

    How do you usually react to them?

    How could you be more assertive the next time you communicate with them?

- Think of an aggressive person in your life who uses anger to get their way.

    How do you usually react to them?

    How could you be more assertive the next time you communicate with them?

THE PASSIVE PERSONALITY
Path of Least Resistance

Have you ever said yes when you meant no? Have you ever agreed to do something you did not really want to do? Have you ever given in to someone's demands because you did not want to make them angry or hurt their feelings? If so, then you have participated in the passive form of communication.

Passive means to take the path of least resistance by tuning out, ignoring, avoiding, or backing away and withdrawing from a person or situation rather than dealing with it head-on. Just as most of you can remember times when you used hurt or anger to get your needs met, you can also recall situations where you have been passive. Throughout life, there are times when you will decide it is not worth the hassle, anguish, frustration, time, or energy to deal assertively with a person or situation, so you choose instead to ignore or avoid the problem, often hoping it will just go away. These are your passive times.

WHAT ARE SOME EXAMPLES OF PASSIVE BEHAVIOR?

Following are some typical real-life situations where people have chosen to be passive and avoid the issue rather than be assertive.

"My friend always wants me to go with her to the movies. I can't stand the movies because they are so crowded. I don't know

95

what to say, so I just go with her anyway, but I hate every minute."

"My coworker loves to gossip about other people at work—employees, customers, and even our boss. I don't add anything to the conversation, but I don't tell her to stop because she might get mad."

"My mom expects us to have dinner at her house every Sunday night. Sometimes, my husband is busy or the kids have plans, but I don't want to hurt her feelings, so we all just go anyway."

"My wife hates it when I play golf. I don't see what the big deal is. I work hard all week, and I'm only gone three hours. But it's not worth it to have her mad, so I just quit playing."

"My husband says I don't need to go back to school. I think he just doesn't want to watch the kids one night a week. I knew I would really learn a lot, and it would help me get that promotion at work, but I guess I won't go. I don't want him angry with me."

"My roommate wants me to help him cheat on his test. I could do it easily, but I don't think it's right. However, he's my friend, and I don't want him to fail, so I told him I'd do what I could."

"My son does nothing to help around the house, even when I ask him directly. He always tells me he's too busy. I guess I shouldn't keep giving him his allowance and keys to the car, but I don't know what to do. It's hard enough already."

"The woman I work with is always making personal phone calls on work time, and I have to pick up the slack by dealing with her customers' calls as well as my own. I haven't said anything because it won't do any good, but I'm thinking of quitting my job. It's too hard with her not pulling her weight."

These are just a few examples. Passive means avoidance. In each of these instances, the person was *choosing* not to deal with the situation in an assertive way. In each case, their own life was being affected by that choice. Passives may avoid a confrontation, but in doing so they create a great deal of stress and unhappiness for themselves.

IT SOUNDS AS THOUGH PASSIVES ARE GOOD AT MAKING EXCUSES FOR NOT DEALING WITH A PERSON OR SITUATION IN AN ASSERTIVE WAY.

We are all adept at rationalizing our behavior, especially when we are choosing to be passive.

Have you ever said any of the following?

"What I say wouldn't make a difference anyway."

"I don't want to get involved."

"It would just make matters worse."

"They don't want my advice or help."

"If I just ignore it, it will go away."

"I probably brought this on myself, so I'll just let it go."

"I'm out of here in a few months. Why cause a problem now?"

"What could I do? I'm just one person."

"I have enough to deal with. They can handle their own problems."

People with passive personalities love to tell themselves that their input does not matter, so they might as well avoid the issue. Passive personalities even make excuses when someone is treating them badly. Rather than place the blame on the aggressive manipulator, they often blame themselves saying, "It must be me. Something I did caused this to happen." It is easy to see why aggressives love to work with, be friends with, and marry passive people. The passive plays right into the aggressive's hand and allows them to be in constant control. For example,

Aggressive: "Where do you want to go?"

Passive: "You choose. Anywhere is fine with me."

Aggressive: "What do you want to do?"

Passive: "Oh, it doesn't make any difference. I'll enjoy doing whatever you want to do."

Passives make it so easy for aggressives to get their own way by giving the aggressive's favorite answer, "I'll do whatever you want to do." They would rather let others make the decision so they do not have to be responsible if things do not work out right. For example, if a passive picks a restaurant and the food or service is poor, their fear is someone might be angry. Then, the passive will feel it was their fault. Rather than be blamed, the passive usually says, "It's just easier to do what everyone else wants. That way, no one will be hurt or angry."

WHY DO PASSIVES HAVE A DIFFICULT TIME WITH CONFRONTATION?

There are two main reasons. One reason is that many passives hate the physical feelings they get when they are involved in a confrontation. Whenever anyone is involved in a tense situation, it is normal to have physiological changes take place in the body. Even when we are communicating assertively, it can be stressful if the other person is not cooperating or playing by the same rules. However, what the passive fails to recognize is that many of the physical symptoms often associated with difficult people and situations such as headaches, stomachaches, internal distress, insomnia, or depression, are a result of avoiding those problems or persons, rather than a result of communicating with them in an assertive way. The fear of what might happen if you take a stand, speak up, or face a situation head on, combined with the anger and frustration of *not* speaking up and the resulting self-doubt, is enough to make anyone ill.

Most stress is caused by avoiding problems and people, rather than by dealing with them.

Secondly, many passives come from families dominated by an aggressive parent or caregiver and they learned at a young age that in order to stay out of trouble, they needed to keep their heads down and their mouths shut. Unfortunately, somewhere along the line they learned through experience that responding assertively is unacceptable.

When they were children, they may have heard statements such as "Shut up and do what I say," "I'm your mother and I said so and that's final," "Children should be seen and not heard," "If I wanted your opinion I'd ask for it," or "Who do you think you are? I'm in charge here." These statements quickly teach a child that if you speak up and give your opinion, you will be in trouble. Sometimes the message to be quiet and nonassertive was more than just verbal. The message might have been accompanied by punishment or physical abuse. In these instances, the children learned that assertiveness was not only unacceptable, but dangerous as well.

Children in these environments learn to adapt a passive stance in order to survive. They learn that if they simply "fade into the woodwork" or just go along, they have a better chance of staying out of harm's way. Something as innocent as direct eye contact, let alone a question or contradiction, could be misinterpreted as impudence and result in serious consequences. Expressing their opinion might easily cause an explosion of feelings that far exceeds what the situation warrants. Sometimes these children never even attempt to speak out because they have watched what happens when others around them (such as older siblings) attempt to be assertive. In these instances, a child is quick to play the game of "whatever you want is fine with me" in order to avoid a negative reaction.

It does not take much for a child to figure out what will happen if they act or respond assertively. When Vicki and I were teaching high school, we would often run into students who had difficulty asking questions or commenting in class. We would find out later that a parent or teacher had made it clear that they were to do as they were told with no questions asked. Sadly, those students learned to be passive—do not speak up or draw attention to yourself and you will stay out of trouble. Unfortunately, a few traumatic instances can sometimes convert an individual into a lifetime of passive behavior, unless the person consciously *chooses* to relearn new assertive techniques and break the passive cycle of childhood. Hard as it may be to change old patterns and habits, it still remains their choice to continue to withdraw and seek peace at all costs or to move ahead and become a vital, confident partner in healthy, assertive relationships.

DID ALL PEOPLE WHO USE PASSIVE AS THEIR MAIN STYLE OF COMMUNICATION GROW UP FEELING IT IS DANGEROUS TO SPEAK OUT?

No. Some passives grew up in environments where just the opposite occurred—they got extra attention for being "such a good child." These children did not necessarily experience any negative reactions to their earlier childhood attempts to be assertive, but instead received a positive reaction that rewarded their passivity. They may have heard the following:

> "What a good little girl you are—you never cause a fuss."
> "You are so nice. I can always count on you not to create any problems."
> "Thank goodness you aren't like your sister and always in trouble."

They learned that the quickest, most effective way of earning the attention and love we all need and want was to not make waves. Perhaps they had siblings who excelled in intelligence, artistic talent, or athletics, and they simply could not compete with those attributes. Instead, their survivalist self discovered that always going along, being good, and doing what everyone else wants merits lots of positive attention. These children do not avoid confrontation because they are afraid, but rather because they have learned to enjoy the attention and praise that comes with always being the good guy and the pleaser. These individuals are not avoiding negative repercussions, but are expecting to bask in the positive limelight.

Both negative and positive reinforcement can change how we perceive ourselves and subsequently alter the choices we make as adults. There is no doubt, however, that most passives grew up either being afraid to speak out or being rewarded for keeping quiet. This pattern usually continues throughout their lives unless they make a conscious decision to change the way they communicate. The consequences and rewards for being nonassertive are persistent and powerful and may cause even the most confident person to question their willingness to confront and deal with difficult people and situations.

DOES THIS MEAN THAT GOOD CHILDREN WILL GO THROUGH LIFE PASSIVELY STRUGGLING TO BE ASSERTIVE ADULTS?

Not at all. But, if the majority of their positive attention as a child came from simply being "good" rather than balanced with their other qualities, talents, and accomplishments, then the lifelong need to stay good in order to be loved, liked, and respected will often take precedence. Sadly, most passives confuse being good with giving in and giving up no matter what toll it takes on their self respect.

SHOULDN'T WE ALL STRIVE TO BE GOOD?

Perhaps this is the time to define exactly what is meant when we refer to a *good* person. When we speak of a good person, let's think of a person who makes consistent, healthy, ethical, and legal choices. Sometimes, being good means saying no, setting limits, enforcing consequences, and even severing unhealthy and destructive relationships. These steps may not always feel good to the other person, but are necessary in order to maintain healthy relationships.

A predominantly passive person often confuses setting limits and saying "no" with being a bad person. Therefore, they are easy prey for aggressives who readily use the threats of guilt and intimidation to reinforce the passive's fear of not being a good person. Unfortunately, passive people are usually very nice people who are often frustrated and saddened by how they are treated and taken advantage of by other people, including those they love and care about the most. They have difficulty understanding that it is their constant commitment to goodness and niceness at all costs that often triggers the mistreatment, disrespect, or even abuse.

---

*Aggressives like to push others to the limit
to see just how much they can get away with.
Passives often fail to set any limits at all.*

Passives must learn to respect themselves first and foremost before they will ever experience true, healthy, and trusting relationships. They must understand and believe that even a good person must set fair and consistent limits. A good person must say "no" at times. A good person has a right to get their own needs met. A good person should expect fair, decent, and respectful treatment. A good person can get assertively angry and express those emotions. A good person does not always have to put everyone's needs before their own. Assertive is a good way to treat and communicate with others. A good person must have high self-esteem and love themselves before they can care for and love others.

HOW IS A PERSON'S SELF-ESTEEM AFFECTED WHEN THEY USE THE PASSIVE STYLE OF COMMUNICATION ON A CONSISTENT BASIS?

Regardless of the reasons, passives generally struggle with serious issues of self-esteem. Earlier, we defined both *self-esteem* and *goodness* as the ability and willingness to make consistent, healthy, ethical choices. This was not a coincidence. There is no doubt that our self-esteem and self-respect are totally connected to our goodness and our commitment to treat others *and* ourselves with respect. When we continually make unwise, unethical, hurtful, or self-destructive choices, our self-esteem plummets. As a result, it is difficult for us to be good to anyone or good for anyone.

Assertiveness, you will recall, requires a great deal of confidence in oneself and the belief that one deserves to be treated fairly and respectfully. Passives rarely give themselves that much credit. Because they are constantly working to put others first, coming in last becomes a way of life: It is the only slot left. They will insist, "But I don't mind. I'm just trying to be nice." That is a wonderful attitude for us to have once in awhile, but on a daily basis, one may become more of a martyr than a truly good person.

Remember we talked about two kinds of nice—nice at any cost and assertive nice? Well, passives have completely bought into the strategy of nice at any cost. They believe, despite all the evidence to the contrary, that if they are always nice (which to them means avoiding issues and confrontation), then people will always be nice to them in return. Unfortunately, that is not what happens when dealing with an aggressive. An aggressive views passivity as a green light for increased manipulation. This can become a very unhealthy pattern. Whereas the passive is trying so hard to be nice, the aggressive begins categorizing them as weak and easily manipulated. Then, the aggressive ups the ante, becoming even more difficult. Passives, rather than putting a stop to the situation, work even harder to avoid a confrontation, perhaps even blaming themselves for the escalating tension. They again try to please and placate the aggressive, and the pattern repeats itself over and over again.

No wonder the passive's self-esteem is low. They are making consistent choices to be dumped on, taken advantage of, ignored, or even mistreated.

You will often hear passives say things like the following:

"It's not fair."

"I don't deserve to be treated this way."

"Why can't we just get along?"

"I didn't do anything wrong."

"Why are you doing this to me?"

"You don't treat anyone else this way."

"When I was a child, I was never allowed to treat my parents the way you treat me."

"I try so hard to be a good wife (dad, employee, etc.), how come this happens?"

I am always suspicious of someone who keeps talking about how hard they are *trying* to be nice. Although there are times when it will take everything you have to stay rational and assertive, you should not have to constantly work to be nice in most situations. Assertive-nice occurs naturally when people value themselves and others. Assertive-nice should not be a forced emotion, but a way of life.

Sometimes you will hear a passive say, "I just can't take anymore," but they inevitably do take more . . . and more and more, sure that one day this unjust world will recognize their self-sacrifice. Many passives could earn the prize for being the biggest martyrs on earth. If you catch yourself expecting a memorial plaque acknowledging your goodness, or regularly saying any of the phrases listed previously either aloud or to yourself, read this chapter carefully: You may be a passive, one of those living saints who is nice at any cost—and the cost is generally your self-respect, physical well-being, and probably your sanity.

I am not saying that it is not good and admirable to be nice, but it is equally important to remember you pay a high price for being nice at any cost. Assertives have the capacity to respect others' feelings without putting themselves last. This seems to be a skill that passives lack. We must all be good to ourselves, not selfishly or vainly, but in a respectful way. What a great truth: In order for us truly to love others, we must love, respect, and believe in ourselves.

Remember: No one will treat us better
than we feel we deserve to be treated.

HOW CAN WE OVERCOME THE NEGATIVE MESSAGES WE MAY HAVE RECEIVED AS CHILDREN SO THAT WE CAN BECOME MORE ASSERTIVE ADULTS?

The bottom line is that no matter what happened in your past,

---

We all have the power to make our own choices as adults, and we
have the obligation to assume responsibility for these choices.

The significant difference between us and other animals is our ability to reason and make choices about how we behave. We can choose to reject what has happened in the past or we can choose to get help and break the cycle. I am not saying that it is easy or that we can just walk away from our past experiences, but we can accept them for what they are: experiences. Our experiences can *influence* who we are, but they do not *define* who we are. Often during counseling sessions, clients would say to me, "I am a battered woman," or "I am a child of an alcoholic." I would tell them, "That is not *who* you are. Those are things you have experienced. Those experiences have had an impact on your life, your attitude, and your beliefs, but you can control and change those feelings. You can replace your old, negative experiences with new, healthy experiences."

You may have experienced things in your life over which you have had no control, but you *can* control how you allow those experiences to define you as a person.

We will have to work hard at understanding how the past has influenced us if we want to change, move ahead, and make new choices. We must all become more conscious of our past if we want to improve our future, especially if we are to have any hope of changing our attitudes and behaviors.

Assertive behavior results from a conscious decision to make healthy choices even when it would be easier to fall back into old patterns of giving up or giving in to the unhealthy influences that pollute our personal histories. Assertiveness takes us out of the passive "victim" role and thrusts us into the I-am-responsible-for-my-actions role—a role that is uncomfortable for many people. After all, shifting the blame to other people can be a great escape from the reality of self-evaluation. Just think for a moment about how much blame is spread around today.

"It's not my fault."

"No one told me."

"Hey, it's not my job."

"Don't look at me. I didn't do it!"

Being assertive requires a great deal of self-reflection on our part and a willingness to explore our past and work hard to change our future. But, we must first believe that we do have a choice about how we live our life and that we *can* break unhealthy cycles and patterns from our past so we can create a totally new and healthy road for our children to travel.

THE WORD *CHOICE* MAKES IT SOUND SO EASY. I DO NOT ALWAYS CHOOSE THE THINGS THAT HAPPEN TO ME.

True. Many things are out of our control—accidents and disasters, for example. But, even in these areas, we can take an assertive role rather than a passive one. We do not have to live in a disaster prone area. We do not have to drink and drive. We can plan ahead and be as educated and prepared as possible just in case we lose our job. And, we can be more assertive in figuring out a solution or plan of action after a crisis happens in our lives. The problem is that passive people seldom take charge and plan ahead. They tend to be more pessimistic saying, "Well, what happens, happens." Passive people spend countless hours, days, and even years blaming their situation on other people or situations.

Assertive is about taking control of your life. Passive is about letting go of control and handing it to others.

Many times when we are faced with situations that we did not actually choose to happen, the only way to regain control of our life is to decide how we will react to these situations.

Assertive communication requires one to be proactive rather than reactive to other people. Assertiveness takes us out of the passive role that says there is nothing you can do or say that will change the pattern of communication you have with another person or the quality of that relationship and thrusts us into the I-am-responsible-for-my-actions (assertive) role that says you alone can change how you choose to react to those around you. The role of "I am responsible" may be uncomfortable for some people. After all, blaming others, making excuses, or avoiding confrontation often seem the easiest way to avoid dealing with difficult people and situations. However, as you will soon learn, these are only short-term answers to long-term problems. As you will see in the following chapters, learning to communicate assertively is the only way to sustain functional, healthy, and happy relationships in all areas of our personal and professional life.

The bottom line is:

You are not to blame for what your early caregivers did or did not do to you as a child. That was not your choice.

However:

No one else is to blame for what you choose to do with the rest of your life as an adult—that is your choice.

Assertiveness is not about blame. Assertiveness is about taking control and being responsible for your choices. There is no room for victims in the role of assertive communicator.

I RECENTLY LOST MY JOB DURING A COMPANY MERGER. THAT CERTAINLY WAS NOT MY CHOICE. HOW COULD BEING MORE ASSERTIVE HAVE HELPED ME IN THIS SITUATION?

Assertive communication requires one to be proactive rather than reactive to other people. Vicki and I have worked with several companies lately that have gone through a major downsizing that often involved serious layoffs. It is interesting to watch how the people in these situations choose to deal with the change. Some employees choose to be bitter and angry. They develop an attitude of "Ok, fine. So, I don't know if I'll have a job next month or not. I'll come to work, but if you think I'm giving this company one ounce more of me than I have to, you're wrong." They choose to be aggressive.

Other employees choose to be passive and not deal with the situation at all. They come to work, do their job, and go home—same as always. Often, when I counsel or interview someone who has recently lost their job through a downsizing or merger, I ask them, "How long did you know that your job might be in jeopardy?" Usually, they tell me they have been afraid for their job security for several months, since the rumors began. "So what have you been doing in that time," I would ask. They look at me puzzled and say, "What do you mean? What could I do? I just came to work every day as usual and waited to hear what is going to happen to me."

Talk about passively giving up control—this is a great example. Months have gone by, and time has been wasted that could have been assertively used to create an outstanding resume, network with people who have leads to other jobs, or take classes to develop new skills. This would prepare someone for the road to finding the security of a new job if the worst should occur. This would not be disloyal to your current company. We are not suggesting you do any of this on paid, company time. As long as the company is paying you a full day's wages, then you owe them a full day's work, but it is not disloyal to keep your options open. In fact, that is exactly what most companies are doing—keeping their options open. A successful company in today's global, competitive environment is always looking to restructure and reformat their strategic plan so they can best serve their customers and their shareholders. It is assertive to prepare oneself to meet those challenges.

Employees who choose to be assertive continue to do a great job, hoping to be part of the team selected to stay on after the merger or restructuring, *but* they also keep their eyes and ears open for other career opportunities. The assertives keep their skills updated and are wise enough to have a resumé ready and waiting if the worst happens. None of the employees can choose to keep their job, but they can choose how they react to a bad situation that is beyond their control.

IS IT PASSIVE TO BELIEVE IN LOYALTY AND EXPECT A COMPANY TO FOLLOW THROUGH ON THEIR SOCIAL CONTRACT THAT SAYS IF I COME TO WORK AND DO A GOOD JOB, THEN I CAN COUNT ON LIFETIME EMPLOYMENT AND A GOOD PENSION WHEN I RETIRE?

Not only is it passive, but it is ignorant. As my coauthor Jean Gatz and I state in our book, *How to be the Person Successful Companies Fight to Keep*, the only institution that can guarantee lifelong benefits is a federal/state prison. No company can guarantee lifelong employment, and no assertive, responsible person will count on that anymore. Employees cannot be passive about their health benefits, savings, and investments, or their pension and retirement. Employees must be assertive, take control, and plan for their future themselves.

WHY WOULD SOME PEOPLE CHOOSE TO PASSIVELY REMAIN IN A SITUATION WHERE THEY ARE TREATED BADLY OR EVEN ABUSED?

An abuser cannot abuse alone. There must be a recipient of that abuse. As we discussed before, sometimes the recipient is not a willing participant—we refer to them as victims. A *victim* is a person who in no way chooses to be a part of the abusive situation. If the abuse is criminal, the victim has a right to press charges for assault, harassment, and so forth. In other situations, however, there is a person who *does* choose to remain with the abuser in the relationship, whether it is a marriage, friendship, or job. This abuse is not a random act of violence—it is consistent and relentless. It could very well be criminal, and yet the abused rarely presses charges. If they do press charges, they often change their minds after the abuser whines, pleads, apologizes, and begs for forgiveness saying, "It will never happen again."

I can remember speaking to a group of women who had experienced being beaten and asking them the question many people want to ask women (and men) in their situation, "Why do you stay and continue to be abused?" Their first answer usually was, "I love him." It always amazed me how much people would put up with and still use the word *love*. The feeling of love should be a result of mutual respect, caring, and trust. When I would ask, "You love him?" their response was, "Oh, but he isn't always like this. Sometimes our relationship is really good. I just try not to say or do anything that I know sets him [or her] off." (Note: Men are not the only ones who abuse. I counseled plenty of abused men whose wives were mean, threatening, hostile, and violent.)

There's that word *try* again. What an effort it must be to always have to worry about making someone angry. I do not believe that this is really love. In the 1970s movie "Love Story," the famous line was, "Love means never having to say you're sorry." Well, I do not agree. A loving relationship involves people who can and must admit when they are wrong and have the confidence and courage to apologize. Feelings of love should be a result of feeling safe, respected, trusted, and valued, but I do believe that,

Love means not having to be afraid.

The second reason people give for passively staying in a destructive, abusive relationship was, "I'm staying for the kids." If you are in an addictive and/or abusive situation, please do not ever rationalize that you are doing your children a favor. Our children watch us every day.

Our children watch how we treat others and
how we allow ourselves to be treated.

From these observations, they are learning and deciding how they will treat others and allow others to treat them when they grow up.

Every child has the right to be in a home free from abuse and addiction. In counseling, I worked to get couples to learn to support one another in a mutually respectful relationship so they could avoid the pain of divorce and the effect it could have on their children. In the case of addiction and abuse, however, divorce may be the child's only salvation. I believe that children stand a better chance of becoming healthy, functional, nonaddictive, nonviolent adults if they grow up in the presence of one healthy, functional, nonviolent, nonaddictive parent, than they do in a home with two dysfunctional adults— one addict or abuser and one equally destructive, silent, passive partner. It may be only one parent who is the addict or abuser, but the other parent stands passively by and *allows* it to continue. This could very well be passivity at its worst.

One very important message to remember at this point is that,

A child may never forget the abusive parent,
but they may never forgive the other one.

In the child's mind, they may never understand or forgive the parent who was supposedly functional and healthy enough to stop the negative behavior and/or abuse and instead stood by and allowed the abuse to continue.

This brings up a third reason why people stay in destructive relationships: They are afraid to leave—afraid of losing their reputation, job, children, or even their lives. This is, unfortunately, a very valid fear for thousands of people every day. The decision to leave a situation when you are afraid requires the highest degree of assertiveness. The problem is that assertiveness requires self-confidence, and people in abusive situations lose a piece of their self-esteem every day they continue to make unhealthy, self-destructive choices for themselves and their children. Please always remember that,

---

If you are afraid to leave a person or situation,
it is usually more risky to stay.

The first assertive choice you must make if you are in a situation where you are afraid of another person is to get professional help. There are agencies and organizations in every community that will support you and direct you so you may begin to turn your life around.

MY SPOUSE IS AN ALCOHOLIC AND CAN BE VERY VERBALLY ABUSIVE AND OCCASIONALLY, PHYSICALLY ABUSIVE, BUT I REALLY WANT TO MAKE THIS MARRIAGE WORK. WHAT SHOULD I DO?

The first thing anyone must recognize when they choose to remain in a relationship with an addict (to drugs or alcohol) is that there is no marriage. It does not make any difference if there is a marriage license or what words or vows were said at a ceremony. The truth about living with an addict is:

It is impossible to be married to an addict because
they are already married ... to their substance.

That substance will consume all of their time, energy, humor, creativity, money, *and* sap you of most of yours. The relationship between a person and their addiction is the strongest marriage in the world. Unfortunately, I have yet to meet the human being strong enough to break up that marriage. If you are living with an addict, your role is really that of a mistress. You will only get their attention when their real "partner" has been satisfied. A person must divorce their partner of substance before they can be an intimate, viable participant in a marriage with another person.

ARE PEOPLE WHO REMAIN IN AN ABUSIVE SITUATION CONSIDERED VICTIMS?

Not by the true definition of a *victim*: one who is harmed or is killed. However, judging by much of the media we see, hear, or read, it appears we have become a world of victims. In the evening news and the morning paper, there is an abundance of tragedy. Many of these people are true victims—people who had absolutely *no* choice about what happened to them and who did not contribute in any way to their situation. These people may be victims of muggings, murders, assaults, abuse, neglect, and other crimes against persons or property.

It is not unusual to find out that perpetrators of these tragic events are also victims. Those who commit crimes are often victims of abusive parents, broken homes, drugs, poverty, and teenage gangs. The problem is that many victims use their past experiences and trauma as a rationale for unacceptable, destructive, unethical, illegal, and/or criminal behavior. In fact, the label "victim" is often used as a courtroom defense as though it were a license to do whatever one pleases and escape the consequences. We read stories daily about people who have committed criminal acts, yet escape penalty by pleading they were victims of a neglectful, abusive family or society.

ARE SOME PEOPLE REALLY PROGRAMMED BY THEIR ENVIRONMENTS IN SUCH A WAY AS TO BE PREDESTINED TO BEHAVE ANTISOCIALLY?

This is an important question because if you believe that behavior is totally predetermined by environment, then you may never believe you have the ultimate power to determine how you act, react, and behave in life. As a therapist, I will admit that far too many people have had atrocious lives full of abuse, neglect, or trauma, but that alone does not make them act outside the norms of acceptable behavior. If that were true, every abused person would turn out to be a criminal, drug addict, or child abuser. Plenty of people have overcome traumatic backgrounds and have become decent human beings with loving relationships, successful careers, and meaningful lives. And, conversely, many people with happy, functional childhoods have become difficult adults who make unethical or illegal choices.

Having been a victim at some point does not give anyone the right or excuse to mistreat or abuse another person.

WHAT ABOUT PEOPLE WHO FIND THEMSELVES IN A DESTRUCTIVE OR ABUSIVE SITUATION AT WORK?

Again, you should never have to be afraid of your spouse, parent, child, or boss. Abuse in the workplace can take all forms from ridicule, sarcasm, and put-downs, to neglect, threats, coercion, and even bodily harm.

At work, you have the right to be treated respectfully and paid fairly. You have the right to understand what is expected of you and to be evaluated on a consistent basis. You have the right to have your opinion and ideas heard and considered without fear of retribution. You have the right to learn and grow. Also, (and here is where responsibility comes in) you have the right to make the assertive choice not to work for a company or employer that does not adhere to these basic employee rights.

If you are experiencing any form of abuse at work, do *not* remain passive. Be assertive and contact the appropriate department within your company such as human resources, employee assistance, or personnel, as soon as possible. If, unfortunately, these departments are unable to help you, go outside of the company and contact your local or state agencies that will educate, counsel, or even defend your right to fair and equal treatment.

Some of you, however, are not being abused. You are just being treated disrespectfully. You still have the choice to leave.

Some of you may be saying, "Well, it's not as easy as it sounds. I can't just quit my job." You might give one or several of the following reasons:

1. I have a family to support.
2. I don't have any other skills.
3. I don't want to move.
4. My savings and retirement are tied up with this company.
5. I don't want to deal with the hassle.

You are right. Making good, functional choices is not always easy. Maybe you cannot quit today, but you can quit at some point in the future. Develop a plan and be assertive. Decide what you need to do (go back to school, learn a new skill, network, send out resumes, rearrange your finances, etc.) so that you *can* leave and find another job you like where you are treated the way you deserve, even if it takes months to put that plan into action.

WHAT ABOUT PEOPLE WHO ARE NOT IN AN ABUSIVE OR DESTRUCTIVE SITUATION, BUT JUST SEEM TO HAVE A PROBLEM SAYING "NO!"

Saying "no" is difficult for many of us at times. Saying "No" can cause some people to feel guilty or anxious. The predominantly passive person usually avoids saying the word and simply chooses instead to go along.

As a rule, passives are afraid that if they state their needs or say how they feel, they will either

1. Hurt someone's feelings

   or

2. Make someone angry

Isn't that interesting? Aggressives use hurt and anger to get their own way, whereas passives try everything in their power to avoid hurt and anger. No wonder passives are such easy prey for aggressives. The passive's fear of hurting someone or making them angry creates several ineffective strategies for dealing (or not dealing) with the world. For instance, the passive person usually has an almost pathological fear of expressing and being around anger. They are disappointed in themselves when even the most mundane irritation arises within or around them. They usually feel most comfortable

and at ease when everyone around them is happy and problem-free. Because people are seldom always happy and problem-free, the passive may then go into denial and simply pretend there are no problems. Passives function best when in a make-believe world where everyone gets along all the time and confrontation can always be avoided. Physically, the passive is often exhausted; mentally, the passive is waging an internal battle; and emotionally, the passive is on edge. That is the price one pays to avoid hassles and problems. It definitely takes a toll on the person who is continually trying to please everyone all the time.

GIVE AN EXAMPLE OF HOW SOMEONE WHO CANNOT SAY "NO" CAN GET INTO TROUBLE AT WORK.

Passives avoid saying "no" in order to be "nice" and usually end up in trouble. For example, a secretary gets requests from three different people in her office who each want her to finish their reports by 5 p.m. She does not want to say "no" because she is afraid she will either disappoint them or make them angry, but neither can she meet their demands and complete all the assigned work accurately and on time. Nonetheless, she passively agrees to do all three reports so she can avoid creating a problem. Of course, she fails: One report is not complete, and the other two are full of errors. She is physically tired from trying to meet unfair demands, and she is mentally battling with herself. She moans, "It's not fair. Everyone in the office takes advantage of me. Why does everyone treat me this way?" (Notice that the secretary blames others for her plight, rather than choosing to take responsibility for her own unwillingness to be assertive.)

All her efforts to please everyone were to no avail. The secretary ends up with everybody angry or disappointed, which was exactly what she wanted to avoid, all because she was "just trying to be nice." The truth is that she was not being nice at all. Nice is not letting people think they can count on you when they cannot. Instead, she was avoiding the issue and, as a result, caused problems for everyone involved. But most of all, she created serious headaches for herself. The sad thing about passives is that in their attempt to avoid anger, they generally end up making everyone angry, including themselves. And, in their attempt to avoid hurting others, they end up disappointing the same people they wanted to help. Passives are continually surrounded by people who behave in the manner they are trying desperately to avoid. By not saying "no," and setting limits, passives hurt and anger the people around them—just what they did not want!

The secretary could have handled the situation far better by being assertive. She could have said, "Ladies and gentlemen, you have each asked me to do a report for tomorrow. This is about 7 hours of work, and I only have 5 hours. I can compromise the quality and rush each one, or I could do two for tomorrow and a third on Monday. Another option is that I can pull in some temporary help and have them all done professionally and accurately today. Which option would you like me to pursue?"

Notice, there is no meanness or anger in that response. It is possible to be assertive *and* nice at the same time. She simply made an honest statement identifying the choices and the consequences of each option. Giving others the alternatives and laying out the situation is far nicer than agreeing to do a job that cannot and will not get done right.

IF SOMEONE IS SHY AND QUIET, DOES THIS MEAN THEY ARE PASSIVE?

No, not necessarily. Not all assertive people are vocal, high-energy, and talkative. *Passive* is about being afraid to speak up. *Assertive* is about not being afraid to speak up, but it does not mean one has to be continuously verbal. Vicki and I have employees in our workshops who are quiet, but yet are never afraid to ask questions when necessary or offer an opinion when appropriate. These quiet, nonverbal employees are also very capable of confronting and standing up to someone if and when they feel something is wrong. In fact, some assertive people are not overly talkative because they take the time to weigh what they are going to say. Assertives are also good listeners, which requires one to be quiet in order to hear what others are saying.

On the other hand, there are plenty of loud, talkative people who are predominantly passive. They talk a lot, but tend to agree with what the majority is saying rather than form their own opinions. These people can be very frustrating, especially if you are counting on their support. You think they are in agreement with you on your ideas and assume you can rely on them, only to discover that they have been equally supportive of an opposing view or opinion.

With a passive, you can never assume they are on your team. They tend to agree with whomever is talking at that moment. The only way to deal with this passive behavior, if it is important for you to know where they stand, is to get their support or vote in writing. A passive's verbal vote of confidence may only be the words they thought you wanted to hear.

ARE PASSIVES MORE SUSCEPTIBLE TO PEER PRESSURE?

Without a doubt, the more passive one is, the more one is worried about how they are perceived by others because they do not want to make anyone angry or hurt anyone's feelings. They may go along with the crowd to avoid those issues. Teaching our children to be assertive is a necessary life technique that not only provides them with the ability to face and deal with difficult times, people, and situations but also gives them a skill that could perhaps save their life. When faced with dangerous or destructive options, it is not easy to "just say no" without an understanding of manipulation and the games aggressives will use to get someone to do what they want.

We must teach and model assertive communication skills to our children along with a working knowledge of the other three styles so they can recognize quickly when they are being manipulated or coerced. Let's never forget that giving in to peer pressure does not stop at adolescence. Many adults face the same situations in their place of business, organizations, or social groups. Aggressives thrive on their ability to make passives feel uncomfortable, as though they would be causing a problem if they refuse to go along with the group.

Peer pressure is about manipulation (aggressive)
and the inability to say no (passive).

HOW DO PASSIVES GET THEIR NEEDS MET?

This question should be, "*When* do passives get their needs met?" The answer is seldom, because passives are often unable to ask for what they need without feeling guilty. In their universe, asking for something for themselves is selfish, which does not fit the pattern of a nice person in their minds.

Passives often play another game, which sounds like this: "If people loved me (respected me, liked me, cared for me, etc.), they would know how I feel and what I need." Passives initiate the game of "let's see if you can guess what I want" and then feel sad, hurt, or let-down when others do not have the ability to read minds. Passives are always trying to figure out what everyone else needs, so, therefore, they expect others to do the same for them. Passives are often very intuitive people. They have a knack for sensing what others want and providing it for them before they ask. The problem is, the passive person expects others to be equally as intuitive, which is not the case. We often refer to this passive behavior as *testing*. The passive is always testing the people they are in a relationship with to see if the other person can guess what they want without them having to ask. They evaluate and grade people on their ability to read the passive's mind. No wonder the passive feels disappointment so often. Not many people are able or willing to guess what someone else wants or needs. Aggressives do not particularly care what others want and assertives, on the other hand, do not presume to read minds because they expect others to say what they want in a mature, grown-up fashion.

Passives and aggressives do have one thing in common: They lack the self-confidence needed to be open, honest, and assertive with the people in their lives. Passives give in, and aggressives dish it out—neither of which helps them develop healthier relationships.

WHY CAN'T PASSIVES BE FIRMER IN THEIR CONVICTIONS AND SET LIMITS?

Passives think the only alternative to being nice is to be mean or selfish. If we believe that nice and mean are our only two choices, no wonder nice wins out! The passive person seldom considers the healthy alternative of communicating assertively. Assertive people work hard to help others get their needs met without sacrificing their own needs. On the other hand, the passive's strategy is to attend to everyone's needs except their own, which encourages people to take advantage and manipulate them.

Sustaining assertive, successful personal relationships requires the ability to set boundaries. Boundaries are the limits each of us set for how others treat us, talk to us, and behave around us based on the principles we have set for fair, ethical, and just behavior. Assertive people maintain healthy boundaries, which sometimes means they have to confront those who violate their healthy physical, psychological, and emotional space. From humanity's beginnings, we have had to defend our boundaries, thus keeping ourselves and our families safe from attack. Unfortunately, setting boundaries conflicts with the passive's approach. If one's goal is to live without confrontation, then it will be impossible to set and enforce boundaries. Setting limits requires us to deal with confrontation and communicate assertively with people who would like to control or manipulate us.

Choosing to go through life passively allows difficult people to move in and take over. Before long, you will have lost what is rightfully yours. When we give up our personal rights, we will inevitably harbor some internal, intense feelings: anger, resentment, sadness, shame, guilt, and grief, to name a few. To avoid the fight on the outside, passives begin an internal battle that could be more destructive than any confrontation they could ever imagine.

PLEASE EXPLAIN THE TERM BOUNDARIES IN MORE DETAIL.

It is worth repeating because boundaries are the cornerstone that must be in place in order for any relationship to be healthy. *Boundaries* are the limits you set that determine how you will treat and be treated by others. These boundaries are a reflection of your basic core beliefs and principles.

Setting boundaries means identifying healthy and ethical principles upon which to base your life and making sure that how you treat others and are treated by others is within the framework of those principles.

For example, if you are predominantly assertive, your life is based on principles such as respect, compassion, freedom, honesty, fairness, equality, and empathy. How you communicate and behave and how you allow yourself to be treated is directly influenced by these values. To communicate either aggressively or passively would be in direct conflict with your basic beliefs and principles. The boundaries you set will let others know through verbal and nonverbal clues and behaviors that these core values are an integral part of your life.

On the other hand, if you are predominantly aggressive, your life is based on a different set of values such as power, control, and winning. Your behavior and communication is directed toward meeting those goals. You will justify and rationalize any behavior that helps you get those needs met, even if it involves manipulation.

If you are predominantly passive, it is interesting to note that your basic values are probably the same as the assertive, but there are two differences.

1. The passive person values the assertive principles for everyone *but* themselves. They do not believe they deserve what they work so hard to give to everyone else.
2. In the passive person's futile attempt to be all things to all people, they often fail to live up to the very principles they

work so diligently to model. They avoid saying "no" and take on too much (dishonest). They want others to read their minds without telling them what they need (unfair). They allow themselves to be dumped on, mistreated, abused, or taken advantage of (lack of respect for self).

WHAT BEHAVIOR MIGHT WE EXPECT FROM THE CHILDREN OF PASSIVE PARENTS?

Unfortunately, many consequences result from this give-in-to-everyone, please-everyone, keep-everyone-happy attitude. For instance, passive parents raise a lot of undisciplined, manipulative children who will grow up to be undisciplined, manipulative adults. In fact, passive parents probably are responsible for the creation of more aggressives than any other personality style. Why? Because they let everything slide. They do not set or enforce limits, which is bad enough in the adult world, but can create total havoc in a family where children are learning how they should communicate and behave in later life.

Passive parents hate to say "no," and when they do say "no," they have a hard time enforcing it. In a passive home, children quickly learn that they can lie, throw a tantrum, pout, or just ignore what is being said and get away with it. Children realize at an early age that passive parents are not necessarily the ones in charge, and they quickly learn to enjoy the feeling of power. A child who grows up in a passive environment learns little about assertive communication, negotiation, mediation, and compromise. Instead of learning to communicate and behave within the framework of a solid, healthy structure where they can assertively get their needs met, they learn to connive and manipulate because that is how they can magically turn a "no" into a "yes" and get what they want. They learn, unfortunately, to value the aggressive's creed: the end (reward) justifies the means (manipulation).

IT SOUNDS LIKE PASSIVE PARENTS DO NOT SET THE BOUNDARIES NEEDED FOR A HEALTHY ENVIRONMENT.

Exactly. Passive parents seldom enforce rules when their children cry, "You don't trust me," "I hate you," or "You're mean." (Remember, in the passive's world, you are either nice or mean, and because they never want to be mean, these complaints trigger instant guilt.) The passive parent fails to recognize that the child is simply testing the limits. Children not only need boundaries in order to prepare them for life in society, they want boundaries because they feel most secure when they know what is expected of them. Children intuitively recognize that some structure is necessary in order for people to get along. They look for this structure at home and school. In fact, consistency and fair boundaries are necessary in order for a child to grow up feeling confident and secure. When we give in to a child's demands all the time, we leave the child unprepared for a world that does not submit to every whim and desire—a world in which there are rules, limits, standards, expectations, and consequences.

I remember counseling a 17-year-old youth who had just received his second DUI (driving under the influence) and, for the second time, his dad had gotten the ticket "fixed" so there was no fine, penalty, or even record of the event. The young man seemed sad and angry. When I asked what he was feeling, he said, "My dad doesn't care about me. He didn't even get mad. If this had happened to my buddies, they'd be grounded for life! My dad just acted like it was a big joke and told me how it had happened to him, too, when he was a kid."

Wow! Here is a young man who recognizes that parents are supposed to set limits. Why? To be mean? No, because that is how we show them we love them. Children need discipline.

Discipline can be defined as love plus guidelines.

Discipline is not the back of a hand, a voice in a rage of anger, or empty threats. True discipline is one of the greatest gifts we can give our children. Our desire to help them become respectful, honest, and decent adults is the true reflection of our love. That 17-year-old knew what his dad had forgotten.

Sometimes in our attempt to give children what we did not have, we forget to give our children what we did have.

Speaking of consequences, passive parents often shield their children from the natural outcomes of their actions. Little Tommy does not want to go to school? No problem, Mom will write an excuse. He does not want to do his homework? Dad will do it. What about that science project that should have been started a month ago? Mom will head out the door after a long day and buy poster board and paint. I am not exaggerating when I tell you that Vicki and I saw more science projects done by parents than by students when we were teaching. Past due books at the library? "Oh, don't worry, Honey, Mom will leave her meeting and drive home to get them and bring them to school. I wouldn't want you to get in trouble."

Passive parents spend a great deal of their time rescuing their children from the consequences of their actions. Why? Because of those two repeating fears: They do not want their children to be hurt, and they do not want anyone to be angry with their children. In rescuing their children from the natural outcomes, however, they have set these same children up for failure in later life. We learn to be responsible, self-sufficient, decent people by experiencing both the positive and negative results of our actions. Passive parents have a difficult time understanding that being nice is not always being the most loving in the long run.

WHAT IS WRONG WITH SAVING OUR CHILDREN FROM GETTING IN TROUBLE? AREN'T WE SUPPOSED TO HELP THEM?

Helping children learn to be respectful, conscientious, honest, and compassionate should be every parent's goal, but by consistently rescuing children from the consequences of their behavior, passive parents fail to teach the lessons needed to become an emotionally healthy, assertive adult (not to mention these parents become slaves to their children). Children need a few detentions, a few zeroes for missed homework, a few sloppy science projects that earn the appropriate "F," and a few time-outs on the bench in order for them to understand there are, indeed, consequences for their failure to act responsibly. It is better to learn about consequences when people are young than to grow up thinking they will be magically saved every time they fail to act responsibly.

Unfortunately, passive parents often pass their fear of confrontation to their children. Nothing could be more crippling to our children than to be denied the ability to debate, negotiate, and stand up for themselves. We need those skills, and we need to see them modeled in the home if we are ever to use them effectively ourselves.

ARE THERE OTHER AREAS BESIDES PARENTING WHERE THE PASSIVE STYLE CREATES PROBLEMS?

Most definitely. For example, passive teachers create chaotic classrooms where students run the class, come late, are unprepared, talk incessantly about subjects that are not relevant, and often ridicule other students or even the teacher. The outcome is an environment where no learning takes place. Passive teachers cheat children out of their education and leave them unprepared for a world where knowledge is power. Passive teachers lack the self-confidence needed to create a safe, functional environment for their students. It is not just *what* an educator teaches that is important, but *how* they teach. Vicki and I speak to thousands of teachers and administrators every year, and we always talk about the importance of being assertive and modeling healthy, productive behaviors that students can hopefully integrate into their lives.

Passive managers and supervisors are another problem. First of all, they are always exhausted. They have difficulty delegating because that might mean a confrontation. They excuse tardiness and ignore attendance problems (another confrontation avoided). Passive bosses are manipulated by aggressive employees who know they can get away with coming to work with a negative attitude, gossiping, or not working efficiently.

In our management and leadership sessions, Vicki and I spend a great deal of time working on assertive skills. Employees will, for the most part, model their attitudes and actions after the leaders in their company.

Passive managers do not know how to take charge and be a leader. They worry more about being liked than being respected. They struggle to set boundaries and rules and when they do, they struggle to enforce them. They often excuse their passive behavior by citing some of today's popular buzz words: empowerment, shared leadership, and delegation. Please note that empowerment, shared leadership, and delegation do *not* mean abdicating authority. A leader can and should solicit their team's opinions and ideas, *but* a functional leader realizes that ultimately they are the one who is in charge, and they must have the courage to accept that responsibility.

Keep in mind that if a manager gives away all the power to employees and is in no way affecting the staff's production and level of service, then that manager's job is not necessary. When no one is in charge and no healthy boundaries are set, chaos, and turmoil take over. Sadly, this describes many workplace environments today.

Passive employees, although they may be dependable, have no spark or passion. Because they cannot say "no," they cannot be counted on to follow through because they are always over-worked, over-stressed and over-extended. They seldom take on leadership roles, initiate change, or risk themselves in any way. Their strategy is designed to keep them safe and out of trouble. Unfortunately, in these days of downsizing, companies are looking for people with exactly those traits the passive seeks to avoid: leaders, self-starters, risk-takers, and people who are passionate about what they do and are willing to stand up for what they believe. When the ax falls, it is often a passive head that rolls, crying, "It's not fair. I was always so dependable!"

A healthy organization, whether it is a family, school, company, or community, consists of people acting assertively. Maturing means learning to accept responsibility for our behavior and our choices. Passive adults do a grave disservice to the children, employees, customers, and students in their lives, as well as all the rest of society because they continually create difficult people—individuals who have no boundaries and respect no one.

AREN'T THERE TIMES WHEN NO RESPONSE MAY BE THE BEST RESPONSE?

Most definitely. We must certainly pick our battles in life, especially today when rage seems to be everywhere: in schools, on the roads, in the workplace, and so forth. Even though being assertive is the healthiest communication style, sometimes there are matters that simply need to be overlooked so that we can move on to more important issues.

For example, as my children grew up and became teenagers, I began to overlook a few clothes on the floor or a bed that was not made. In the relationship between teen and parent, there are definitely far more important battles to wage, such as school performance, substance abuse, and respect for oneself and others. The condition of a teenager's room, length of their hair, or style of clothes may not be where we want to focus our energy. (Note: If, however, a parent believes that the hair or clothes reflect friends and a lifestyle that could be threatening or destructive rather than the normal need to distinguish their own identity, then this may indeed be one of the important battles to fight.)

Sometimes in relationships we need to overlook minor annoying traits and concentrate on the overall positive traits of the other person. Assertive does not mean we must constantly confront every little thing we do not like, as long as these minor issues do not compromise our own self-respect. In fact, it is a sign of emotional stability and maturity to be able to tell the difference between those areas that warrant our time and energy and those that do not. From now on, we will refer to healthy avoidance as assertive-passive. When we are maturely and wisely choosing to ignore a situation because it does not warrant our time and energy and does not impose upon our (or others') rights, then our self-esteem remains intact and our actions fall under the heading *assertive*. We do not experience feelings of guilt, shame, or self-doubt when we are being assertive-passive. We are *not* being treated badly or allowing someone else to be treated badly as a result of our decision to ignore or avoid a situation or person.

In fact, there are times when avoidance is not only justified, but applauded. For example, when we are in the presence of a person who is out of control, either physically or emotionally, it may be prudent to back off and avoid a potential conflict at that moment with an irrational person. However, if this person is one with whom you have an on-going relationship, you must figure out how to deal with the situation assertively as soon as you are out of harm's way. If you are consistently having to back off from a difficult person, then your behavior no longer represents the mature choice, but rather the nonassertive, passive choice.

ARE WE BEING PASSIVE AND AVOIDING CONFRONTATION WHEN WE COMPROMISE?

Not necessarily. Compromise does require that we give in or let go of something we want, but a true assertive compromise means that we also gain something at the same time. Often, when *both* parties elect to forgo a battle for the good of the relationship, a stronger alliance emerges.

The trouble for the predominantly passive personality is this: They rarely choose any battle. In fact, a passive personality tends to shy away from almost all confrontation. What they believe to be a compromise is usually giving in with nothing gained or resolved in return, but a sense of loss, shame, frustration, or anger.

When passivity becomes our default response, then we have a problem because not only do we continue to "compromise" with nothing gained, but our ethics and values are inevitably compromised as well. As a result, our self-esteem is diminished.

> Compromising with another person is one thing;
> compromising ourselves is quite another.

Passives are willing to overlook and avoid issues they do not like or do not believe in because the fear of confrontation is greater than the fear of losing their self-respect. Conversely, assertives pick the battles they will pursue. If an assertive avoids a battle or chooses to compromise, it is because after weighing all the options, avoidance or compromise is the best choice and in no way will compromise the beliefs, values, and rights of the assertive.

Passives, however, simply compromise to avoid difficult situations because they fear confrontation. The passive's unwillingness to become involved does not constitute a compromise, but rather capitulation. Their compromise will most likely also compromise some of their basic values and beliefs. This is another inner conflict that passives endure in their attempt to be nice and keep the peace.

HOW CAN I TELL IF PASSIVE IS MY MAIN STYLE OF COMMUNICATION?

It is easy. You do not feel very good about yourself most of the time. You believe that most people take advantage of you or treat you unfairly. You believe that you give much more than you receive. You are waging a constant internal battle: "Do something!—No, I can't!" or "Say something!—No, it's not worth it!" Inside you know what you would like to have said or wish you had done, but the words never materialized. With that kind of internal dialog going on, passive people experience a great deal of frustration, self-doubt, and anger. Unfortunately, the anger is seldom directed at the person or situation that probably deserves those feelings, but inward at themselves. Passive people avoid conflict and confrontation, but then get angry at themselves for not being assertive. Sometimes they even promise themselves that they *will* handle the situation assertively next time, but they rarely follow through. When the next time comes, they usually opt for the passive role again.

Most people who believe they have low self-esteem and say, "I've never had a great deal of confidence in myself," have been communicating in the passive style for a long time. It is nearly impossible to maintain a healthy sense of self-respect when passive is the communication style of choice. Remember, self-esteem is maintained by making consistent, healthy choices. The choice to not deal assertively with difficult people and, as a result, be mistreated, disrespected, threatened, or manipulated is not healthy to one's self or one's relationships.

In the next chapter, we will talk about how to deal with passives. They can prove quite a challenge because the hallmark of their behavior is doing nothing. At least with an aggressive, we have overt behavior we can respond to and thus redirect. What you see is what you get with the aggressive. Nonetheless, there are steps we can take to assure that we have satisfactory relations with the passives in our lives.

Summary

- Passives are intimidated when faced with manipulative anger and feel guilty when faced with manipulative hurt.
- Most stress is caused by avoiding problems and people, rather than by dealing with them.
- Aggressives like to push others to the limit to see just how much they can get away with. Passives often fail to set any limits at all.
- No one will treat us better than we expect to be treated.
- We all have the power to make our own choices as adults and we have the obligation to assume responsibility for these choices.

- You may have experienced things in your life over which you have had no control, but you *can* control how you allow those experiences to define you as a person.
- Assertive is about taking control of your life. Passive is about letting go of control and handing it to others.
- Setting boundaries means identifying healthy and ethical principles upon which to base your life and making sure that how you treat others and are treated by others is within the framework of those principles.
- Compromising with another person is one thing; compromising ourselves is quite another.
- Aggressives enjoy being around passive people because passives allow them to do their own thing, in their own time, in their own way, even if it involves manipulation and/or abuse.
- Passives generally have low self-esteem as a result of making unhealthy, even self-destructive choices.
- Passive people usually avoid saying, "no" in order to be nice.

Take Action

- Think about a time when you chose to be passive.
- Why did you choose to be passive? Were you afraid of hurting someone's feelings? Were you afraid of making someone angry?
- Do you often wish you had said or done something instead of remaining silent? If so, think about communicating more assertively in the future.

7

DEALING WITH THE PASSIVE PERSON

Some of you may be wondering why we need to learn how to deal with passive people. After all, the passives are the saintly, nice, never-cause-a-fuss, I-will-do-whatever-you-want people. Sounds like the kind of people you would like to have around all the time, right? Wrong!

Although it is true that passives are usually considered nice people, they do cause a fuss—constantly! They are frustrating and confusing. They are insincere and vague. They are wishy-washy and unreliable. They do not tell you how they really feel because they are too busy telling you what they think you want to hear or what will keep the peace. They usually take on more than they can handle because they hate saying "no." This is probably not the kind of person you want to be around.

CAN WE HELP THE PASSIVE PERSON LEARN TO BE MORE ASSERTIVE?

Yes, we can. Remember, passives learned to avoid confrontation a long time ago, so it is foolish to think we can create a secure, confident, tell-it-like-it-is person overnight. What the passive person is missing is trust and self-confidence. Passives do not trust us to respond positively to any assertive attempts on their part because that has not been their experience in the past. Also, they lack the self-confidence needed to believe that their own needs and concerns are valid and worthy.

130

Interestingly enough, however, we have the same two problems with passives: We do not trust that they will be honest when they share their feelings and concerns, and we lack confidence that they will follow through and do what they say. Remember:

It is impossible to change another person, but we can change how *we* respond and react to people and situations.

We cannot change a passive person, but we can make sure that our behavior and communication with them creates an environment where they can feel comfortable being assertive. When a passive person does make an attempt to be more open and honest, they need us to respond to their effort with positive encouragement.

As parents, for example, we need to offer positive reinforcement when our children are open and honest with us. That does not mean they will always get their way or that we must even agree with them, but it is important to validate their right to have an opinion as long as it is given assertively and respectfully. Too often, our children's assertive behavior is met with negativity or defensiveness ("How dare you question me!"), which in turn creates passive children who are afraid to speak out.

Also, at work, if an employee normally does not give her opinion, try asking her to share her thoughts about a project you are working on, then thank her for her input. It is important to be assertive with a passive person. Assertive behavior is peaceful and safe to be around. Passives will learn to respond assertively in a healthy environment with our encouragement.

WHEN YOU SAY THAT WE DO NOT TRUST PASSIVES, ARE YOU SAYING THAT THEY ARE LIARS?

Well, basically, yes. They are not liars in a mean, malicious sense, but they continually cover-up or ignore their own feelings and needs in order to avoid a hassle and to appease others or because they do not believe their needs are important, but that is still dishonest. They avoid telling the truth if it means an argument or a confrontation. We cannot have healthy, successful, or happy relationships when we cannot trust others to tell us how they feel, what they need, and what bothers them. It is very difficult to live with, be friends with, or work with someone who does not say what they mean. We are expected to read their minds, and then they are disappointed when we fail to do so. This is not the basis for a healthy relationship.

If the passive senses a confrontation or feels the tension level getting high, they will agree to almost anything to get the situation back on an even keel. As a result, we learn not to trust them or believe what they say. Unfortunately, they do not trust us either; therefore, they are unwilling to open up and share their feelings and concerns. They may think that no one really cares about how they feel even if they did speak up, or maybe they are afraid of getting in trouble. Whatever the reason, passives need a safe, functional environment where they can learn that it is crucial to be open, direct, and assertive if they want to be an integral part of any relationship.

HOW CAN WE DEVELOP MORE TRUST BETWEEN OURSELVES AND THE PASSIVE PERSON?

Getting someone to trust us and learning to trust someone who has misled, exaggerated, or lied to us takes patience and time. Often, the passive person marries, befriends, hires, or works for an aggressive personality. It makes perfect sense—the two personalities dysfunctionally fit together like glue. Aggressives get their needs met through manipulation using hurt or anger, so they are always on the lookout for someone who responds to and rewards these techniques. Lo and behold, along comes the passive. Passives, at all costs, try to avoid making someone angry or hurting someone's feelings. The aggressive yells and the passive backs off. The aggressive acts hurt and the passive feels guilty and gives in. They are a match! The aggressive constantly reaffirms the passive's fear and reluctance to engage in a meaningful, open dialogue where both parties share honest feelings. Every time the passive speaks up, the aggressive moves into action using either hurt or anger and the passive backs off. Then, the passives berate themselves for opening up and saying what they really feel and promise themselves they will keep quiet in the future.

The first thing that must be done in order to develop trust with a passive is to look within yourself. Do you use manipulation (hurt or anger) with the passive people in your life? Even if you are unaware of this happening, it is so easy to do with them because they give in or give up so quickly, rarely letting us ever know they were affected by our behavior or manipulations.

Passives need to experience what it is like to be assertive without making someone angry or hurting someone's feelings. So, if we truly want the passives in our life to shape up, then we must commit to being assertive with them. To begin with, we must avoid manipulation at all costs and help them understand that in their relationship with us, it is all right to share ideas, opinions, and concerns without fear of retribution or manipulation. This will not be a quick process because the passives are most likely surrounded by aggressives in their other relationships. It may take a long time for them to begin to trust you and feel safe sharing their personal feelings and beliefs.

HOW CAN WE HELP THE PASSIVE PERSON BE MORE OPEN AND TRUTHFUL?

Once you have identified someone as a predominantly passive person, then you must try to help them to focus on being as direct and assertive as possible. For example, the following is how an assertive manager would deal with a passive employee:

Manager: "Melinda, both of these projects need to be handled today and both need to be done accurately and professionally. I need to know honestly whether you are comfortable with making that happen. (The manager words his request carefully. He knows from past experience that if he simply asks Melinda to handle a project, she will agree no matter what. Even though she will always work hard and try her best, she often fails to complete the task professionally, in a timely manner, or accurately. Therefore, recognizing her good points, yet aware of her unwillingness to say "no" or disappoint him in any way, he has learned to ask specific questions that will help Melinda be as honest as possible about what she can or cannot do.)

Melinda: "If you need them done, then I'll be glad to work on them."

Manager: "I know you're willing to help, but I need to know if you are totally confident that you can finish both projects in a short amount of time and still complete them as accurately as possible."

Melinda: "Well, I'll most certainly try."

Manager: "I know you'll try, Melinda, but that isn't what I need to know. Are you positive that you can complete both projects accurately and on time?"

Melinda: "Well, I don't really think I can do both as well as I would like unless . . . "

Manager: "Unless what?"

Melinda: "Unless I have some help or stay late."

Manager: "Which of those would you prefer?"

Melinda: "Well, my son has a playoff soccer game, and I'm supposed to drive, but I guess I could . . . "

Manager: "Do you think staying late is the best option?"

Melinda: "Not really. My son is counting on me."

Manager: "Then, what else could you do?"

Melinda: "I could ask Jennifer from the payroll department to help me for an hour. I know she has a light work load today."

Manager: "Good idea. Please call her and arrange that."

Whew! Tiring, huh? But that is what it takes to communicate with a passive person if you want to really know how they feel. You must accept the fact that without this type of prodding they are probably going to agree to whatever you ask, even if they are unsure of the results. Because most of us are rushed and busy, it is tempting to just accept their willingness to help and go along with them at face value, especially if it fits our needs. That is where you will get into trouble, because you can *never* take the passive at their word. We must always remember that they will cover up, even lie about their feelings, in order to keep the peace and please others. It is important, therefore, that we take the time to carefully word our needs so the passive understands that (a) there are options, and we really need them to be honest with us, (b) they can trust us and safely share those honest feelings, and (c) if they really want to avoid a hassle, it would be better to resolve the issue now than to deal with it later.

The manager can now say, "Thank you, Melinda. I appreciate that you told me what needs to happen so both projects can be completed on time." Melinda will begin to see that nothing bad will happen if she tells people what she truly feels. She has admitted she

could not finish the job (which is her worst fear because she might make someone angry or hurt their feelings) and no one acted either hurt or angry. She will now store this information to use in future situations and will be much more likely to be honest with her manager the next time a similar situation occurs. The manager can now relax and trust that Melinda will call in help and make sure that the work is done. Once Melinda feels safe with this manager, the need to react passively will be lessened.

Have you ever had a friend who was passive? Have you known someone who never can make a decision and seldom offers an opinion? Conversations with a passive friend often go like the following:

You: "Hey, Margie, I have Saturday afternoon free. Would you care to go to the movies with me?"

Margie: "Oh, sure! That would be great."

You: "What movie would you like to see?"

Margie: "Oh, I don't care. You pick one."

You: "I picked last time. Why don't you choose this time?"

Margie: "Really, whatever you want to go see is fine with me."

You: "Well, I have been wanting to see Movie B. Does that sound good?"

Margie: "Oh sure. That's fine. See you Saturday!"

The problem is Margie has no desire to see Movie B, but she does not want to cause a problem. So, instead of telling you how she really feels, she does what passives do all the time—she lies! Margie will say she was not lying and that she was just going along to be nice, but internally Margie is either nervous or mad about doing something she does not really want to do. There is no way for you to know all of this is going on. What is really frustrating is after all your efforts to include Margie in your decision, she will now go out and tell people how bossy you are! We need to encourage the passive people in our lives to make some decisions and help carry the load. Next time, try the following approach with your passive friend:

You: "Hey, Margie. Do you want to go to the movies with me Saturday afternoon?"

Margie: "Sure".

You: "What movie do you want to see?"

Margie: "Oh, I don't care. You pick one."

You: "Well, I'd enjoy seeing either A, B or C. I've heard good things about all three, so now it's your turn to pick which of those three you would like to see."

Margie: "Really, I don't care."

You: "Well, then I guess we won't go, because you're my friend, and I don't want to be the one who always makes the decisions. I enjoy doing things you like, too. That's what is nice about being friends. So . . . choose a movie."

Margie: "Well, I did hear that Movie A is pretty good, but I don't know for sure. I don't want you to blame me or be mad if it's not good after all." (See, this is what the passive is afraid of and why they avoid making decisions. They don't want to be responsible if they are wrong.)

You: "Great! Let's try that one. And, Margie, please know that I'm not going to be angry or blame you if it turns out to be a terrible movie. I don't know any more about it than you do. If it's bad, we'll just leave and go have lunch—no big deal. I'm just glad to be able to spend some time with you."

Remember, passive people feel that they need our permission to make decisions and give their input, and they need our praise when they actually do so, and they need to be reassured that if they are wrong, it will be okay. It will not be the end of the world and you will not be angry or hurt. All too often, we complain about the passive people in our lives because they do not speak up, only to complain when they finally do.

WHAT IF I DO NOT WANT TO TAKE THE TIME TO GET TO THE BOTTOM OF WHAT THE PASSIVE IS REALLY TRYING TO SAY?

That is your choice; however, do not get angry, frustrated, or disappointed when the passive does not follow through. The passive is deceiving at first because it seems refreshing in this age of anger, rage, and short tempers to have someone so easy to deal with, but there are some serious drawbacks to the passive's desire to go along at any cost.

To deal successfully with a passive, you *must* teach them by modeling assertive behavior on how to solve problems, sort out options, share concerns, and tell the truth about what is really happening. Anyone who has ever been involved with teaching, coaching, and mentoring knows that these jobs require tact and patience. Those are the skills it takes to successfully deal with a passive person while levels of trust begin to build.

It really is not a question of whether you would like or not like to take the extra time with a passive; it is a necessity if you are to get your own needs met in your relationship with them. Otherwise, you will become disappointed and frustrated when you find you cannot count on them to do what they promised or say what they mean.

WHAT IF I AM NOT SURE HOW ASSERTIVE I WANT THE PASSIVES IN MY LIFE TO BE?

This is an important issue. If we are getting our needs met because a passive gives in and does what we want, then we probably would like to maintain the status quo. How nice to have someone around who will basically do whatever we want with no questions asked. In fact, if there are passive people in your life, it is probably difficult to *not* take advantage of them—they make it so easy. But, please realize that the relationship may not survive because of two reasons.

One reason is that a passive generally becomes very tiring and very frustrating to be around. After a while, you find yourself screaming, "But what do you want to do? Where do you want to go? Can't you ever offer a suggestion or have some input?" It is hard to have respect for someone who rarely has an opinion or idea of their own. Arguments are wasteful, but a good, healthy debate with someone you like and trust can be stimulating and educational. A major part of a healthy relationship is having someone with whom you can share ideas and who you can trust to let you know if you are headed in the wrong direction. If the passive always agrees no matter what, they can quickly change from easy to get along with to dull, monotonous, and unreliable.

If you truly want to keep the passives in your life passive, then it may be fair to assume that you are an aggressive who likes to stay in control. You may be in charge, but please know you will never have a complete, trusting, and open relationship. I have seen relationships between aggressives who want to be in constant control and passives who want to avoid conflict last a long time. Sometimes, both parties appear to be very content in their respective roles, although I always wonder about the passive and how happy they truly are.

Perhaps their outward show of contentment is just part of a lifelong attempt to keep the peace, even at the expense of their own happiness. On the other hand, in most relationships between an aggressive and a passive, the aggressive tends to become more manipulative and sometimes even abusive as time goes on. As we discussed earlier, aggressives only respect assertives who have the self-confidence to stand up to them and their manipulative attempts. Although the aggressive enjoys the feeling of control and power they have over the passive, they begin to lose respect for them early on in the relationship. The aggressive sees the passive's "niceness" as a weakness and becomes more and more aggressive. They push harder and harder, trying to see just how much the passive will take from them. This is not a functional and healthy relationship.

Functional, healthy relationships are not about control and power. An aggressive/passive relationship, which is the most common combination, is all about control and power. Manipulation through guilt and anger are the weapons, and sadness, martyrdom, disappointment, and withdrawal are the end results.

The second reason the relationship may not survive is because passives have a way of turning on you after years of giving up and giving in. They may either become aggressive and use some of the same techniques that always worked on them, or they will find a way to get even—not overtly, but secretly and deviously. This is the communication style called passive-aggressive, which we will discuss in the next chapter.

WHAT IF A PASSIVE NEVER CHOOSES TO BECOME ASSERTIVE NO MATTER WHAT I DO?

In that case, you have a choice to make about this relationship. First, be very honest. Are you really providing a safe, assertive environment where the passive can learn to trust you and feel confident sharing their honest ideas, opinions, needs, and feelings? If so, then you must assess how irritating or damaging their passive behavior is to you and your relationship. If it is simply a matter that they do not want to choose a movie or restaurant because they really do not care, then you can probably live with making most of the minor decisions in your relationship. If, however, their passiveness is affecting you and your life because you cannot count on them or because you truly want a relationship where feelings, opinions, and ideas are shared equally, then you must decide whether to continue the relationship.

If the passive is your boss who cannot give you clear direction, is always wishy-washy about policy, says what he thinks he should say rather than stand up for his beliefs, and will not support you if there is even a hint that it could cause a confrontation, then you have to decide if this is where you want to work. In an age of mergers, layoffs, and downsizing, it is scary to have a passive boss who may be afraid to stand up for you and help fight for your job if the issue is raised. We need to believe our bosses will be our advocates if we work hard and deserve that support.

If the passive person is your employee who cannot say "no," is always overwhelmed, who does not follow through, hides mistakes rather than dealing directly with a problem, or cannot effectively and assertively work with coworkers and customers, then you must decide if this is who you want working for you. In a work environment where teamwork is important, it is vital that employees can trust and count on their coworkers to do their part.

If the passive is your spouse who cannot open up, does not share opinions or ideas, sees every discussion as a potential conflict to avoid, and hates to discipline or set structure for your children, then you must decide whether you can live with their inability to have a truly intimate partnership. Sometimes, however, it is often difficult to justify severing a long-term relationship simply because someone has difficulty communicating openly. The passive is usually a pretty good person who wants to get along and is committed to making others around them happy. Unless their passivity is causing them to act in an unethical or illegal manner, or they are psychologically incapable of having an intimate relationship, it might be worth learning to love them, flaws and all, and enjoy their many good points while doing everything possible to create a trusting environment where they can feel safe being more intimate.

When I was counseling married couples, I rarely suggested that the aggressive leave the passive, but I must admit, I often questioned why the passive stayed and put up with the aggressive. In most cases, when the passive got away from the aggressive, they discovered that they were very capable of communicating assertively. They had just never been given the chance.

However, if the passive is a person who not only has difficulty with confrontation and speaking up, but also lacks the ability to have a complete and intimate relationship both emotionally and physically, then the question must be asked, "Can I continue to be lonely in this marriage?" I always tell my clients that there is a big difference between being alone and being lonely. Being alone can be a gift, a treat, a time to savor and enjoy. It does not have to be sad or depressing. And, we do not have to experience the feeling of loneliness just because we are alone. I encountered many people in my counseling sessions who were lonelier living with someone than they probably would have been if they lived alone. A cornerstone of a good marriage is the commitment to be intimate from both partners (and do not confuse intimacy with sex).

A person can have sex and never experience intimacy. A person can be intimate with someone and never have sex.

Intimacy is about trust and mutual respect and a willingness to share and care.

HOW CAN I HELP THE PASSIVE PEOPLE IN MY FAMILY LEARN TO BE MORE TRUSTING?

The passive parent will usually run to the rescue of every child to avoid all problems, but you must assertively insist that children need to learn about boundaries and consequences. Help your passive partner understand the importance of assertive negative and let them know in a loving way that it is important that your child not fear confrontation, so that the child can deal with future difficult situations as an assertive adult. Perhaps your spouse may need some professional counseling to help them understand their fears, both about themselves and others. There are reasons, often stemming from childhood, why they are afraid to open up and share their own feelings, needs, and concerns. There are also reasons why they are afraid to let their children face the natural consequences of irresponsible behavior and run, instead, to their rescue. They may need help to uncover those reasons.

Passives may welcome the idea of counseling because life has not been easy. Every day for the passive is a struggle to keep the peace. Passives worry a great deal about how they are perceived and what others think about them. They often take things personally that were not even directed at them. It is quite a burden to bear the responsibility of everyone's happiness on a single shoulder. I found many passives eager to come to my office for counseling because, as one said to me, "You are the first person I can tell everything to and not worry about how you'll feel, whether I've hurt your feelings or whether I made you angry."

If the passive is your child, step back and take a long, hard look at your home life. Is it acceptable to share feelings, ideas, and opinions in a respectable way? Are the adults healthy, functional, and assertive so the child has consistent role models so they know how to act and communicate in an assertive way? Or, is there aggressive behavior—manipulation, guilt, fear, and anger—present in the home? Do the adults set healthy boundaries and then use the assertive negative style of communication when necessary to follow through with fair, nonpunitive consequences? If so, the child has a wonderful opportunity to witness firsthand how good, caring people treat one another.

IN SOME AREAS OF MY LIFE, I AM VERY ASSERTIVE, YET IN OTHER AREAS I AM PASSIVE, WHY IS THIS?

Please know that this is normal. Remember, we have all communicated in each of the four styles at some time in our lives, and it is not unusual to have different styles dominate in specific situations or with different people. For example, some of us use one style at work and another at home, or one style with our family and another with our friends, or one style with men and another with women.

Many women, for example, have learned to be very assertive in their professional life. They can fight for an idea, stand up to a difficult client, refuse to just go along with the crowd, and professionally debate an issue that needs to be resolved. Yet, some of these very same assertive, professional women are not proficient at getting their needs met in their personal relationships. They resort to passive techniques and wait for their spouse or significant other to read their minds, get their feelings hurt, and give in rather than have a long-needed discussion where they assertively state their needs and concerns.

Some men, on the other hand, may be very assertive at work. They share the decision making, form teams for consensus, and work to resolve and negotiate problems. Yet, some of these same assertive men resort to old aggressive techniques in their personal relationships. They yell if something does not go their way, go on the attack if they think they are being nagged or questioned, and withdraw and refuse to speak if they feel out of control. To avoid stereotyping, there are also situations where the assertive woman becomes aggressive in the home, or the assertive male uses guilt and martyrdom as a passive, manipulative tool at home.

For the most part, assertiveness seems to be noticeable in professional relationships more than personal relationships for two reasons. First, we are often evaluated on our ability to cooperate as a team member at work, so we have had to integrate assertive techniques in a professional setting. Also, most businesses are teaching assertive skills such as conflict resolution, mediation and negotiation, team building, shared leadership, and empowerment. Remember, most of us did not have many opportunities in our earlier years to experience or learn assertive behavior. So, for many people the assertive team building and communication training they are receiving at work is very valuable and applicable to both their professional and personal relationships.

Second, we often treat the people we work with more patiently and respectfully than we do the people we love. In many family relationships, there have been things said and done that are not easily forgotten or forgiven. Games and manipulation have gone on for so long that it is difficult to recapture the trust needed to be assertive. If this is the case, it is imperative that you do whatever is necessary to reestablish the trust, or the relationship will never be healthy or satisfying.

IS BEING ASSERTIVE THE BEST WAY TO DEAL WITH PASSIVE BEHAVIOR?

Yes. As we stated before, dealing with the passive person most definitely begins with our commitment to be assertive and create an environment of trust. They must trust us to not react to their assertive attempts with hurt or anger. The passive must feel worthy and respected in our presence so that they have the confidence to share their feelings and concerns.

A good question to ask yourself is, "How do others feel in my presence?" An interesting note is that most of the students I counseled who had dropped out of school said they did not feel good about themselves while in school. Also, many employees I counseled who hated their jobs told me that they did not feel good about themselves while they were at work. And, many of the couples I counseled who were in a situation where one partner had had an affair said they did not feel good about themselves in the presence of their spouse. Obviously, how we feel about ourselves in the presence of others has a direct impact on our choice of communication style. Passives thrive in the presence of assertive people. They respond to an environment that is free from manipulation. Most passives have felt guilty for so long and for so many reasons that they often describe feeling "a sense of freedom for the first time" when they are in the presence of an assertive who gives them permission to share their feelings in a safe environment.

Summary

- It is impossible to change another person, but we can change how *we* respond and react to people and situations.
- Passives lack the trust and self-confidence needed to communicate assertively. Passives learn to avoid confrontation.
- You must make time to get to the bottom of what a passive is really trying to say.
- Do not allow passives to make commitments you know they cannot keep.
- You must communicate assertively with passives.
- Passives need to experience what it is like to be assertive without hurting someone's feelings or making someone angry.
- We can help passive people learn to focus on being direct and assertive.
- Give the passive people in your life permission to make a decision, and then praise them for their participation.

Take Action

- Identify two passive people in your life. Think about whether you create a safe, assertive environment in which they can learn to communicate more openly.
- How can you help the passive people in your life trust you and feel more confident about sharing their honest feelings with you?

8

THE PASSIVE-AGGRESSIVE PERSONALITY

Getting Even

I bet there is someone in your life right now who deserves to be taught a lesson. Someone who said something snide about you? Someone who is making your life difficult? Someone who just needs to be knocked down a notch or two? Go ahead, say the name, you are among friends. Are you already planning what you can do to pay them back and even the score? Would you like to get some well-deserved satisfaction and exact a bit of revenge—all without actually confronting the party in question? If the answer is "yes" to any of the above, you are almost certainly going to need a lesson from the passive-aggressive's handbook. Before you do that, let me warn you, it is not likely to turn out the way you want it to. There is good reason why novels cast the revenge-seeking character as the villain and never the hero.

HOW CAN SOMEONE BE PASSIVE AND AGGRESSIVE AT THE SAME TIME?

Passive-aggressive—it seems like a contradiction in terms, doesn't it? We think of aggressive people as forceful and confrontational and passive people as laid-back and nonconfrontational. But, a passive-aggressive person does manage to do both. They appear to avoid conflict and then use that deceptive mask as a forceful strategy to pay us back and make us suffer. Passive-Aggressive behavior can sneak into a relationship whenever someone feels angry, betrayed, jealous, threatened, or intimidated, or maybe when they are being competitive and want to be in control. There is no doubt that passive-aggressive behaviors represent the darker, greedier, and more devious part of one's personality. That is why passive-aggressive is the communication style most likely to destroy a relationship. It is hard to forgive and forget someone who intentionally tries to get their needs met at our expense and does it in such a sneaky way that we do not even know what hit us. We are left feeling used and betrayed.

Like the passive personality, the passive-aggressive personality does not like face-to-face confrontations and avoids dealing with people assertively. Yet, like the aggressive, they enjoy being in control and getting their own way. They are very comfortable using devious strategies to do just that. And, like the aggressive, passive-aggressives are master manipulators, except they are far more subtle when using the tools hurt and anger. They can be so subtle, in fact, that you may never suspect they are waging a secretive war with you at that very moment.

Passive-Aggressives are so sneaky and insidious that they will almost make you thankful to have a few aggressives in your life. At least with the overt manipulators, you know who and what you are dealing with, and that gives you some options. If you know who your opponent is, you can initiate some effective strategies to open the lines of communication and plan how you can most effectively deal with their behavior. The passive-aggressive, on the other hand, hides from view, like a sniper in the trees. When they are in the open, these individuals often play a friendly game, even going so far as to make you think they are your very best friend. Often, they are the last person you would expect to sabotage you. This covertness allows them to get away with reprehensible and cowardly behavior. They do things in such a way that you feel uncomfortable confronting them even when you begin to suspect that there is more going on than meets the eye. If you do ask, "What do you mean by that?" or "Do you have a problem with me or our relationship?," they will just deny everything. "Who me? No way. I'm fine," or they may say, "That's not what I meant." Perhaps you recognize this, "Oh, I was just kidding. What happened to your sense of humor?" Yet, you

know instinctively that there was a hidden message beneath their seemingly innocent comments.

HOW CAN I IDENTIFY THE PASSIVE-AGGRESSIVES IN MY LIFE?

It can be tricky identifying passive-aggressives because they deny their feelings and act one way to your face and another behind your back. For this reason, the passive-aggressive often goes unnoticed while we focus our attention on the more obvious aggressives in our lives. At some point, our intuition takes over and we begin to have a suspicious *feeling* that someone is not quite who they appear to be. Once we become more observant, the subtle and not-so-subtle signs begin to appear.

Although the passive-aggressive does not want a face-to-face confrontation, they usually cannot resist dropping clues that indicate their dissatisfaction with us such as heaving long, heavy sighs; rolling their eyes; shaking their head in mock frustration; and so on. These are usually small clues—in fact, so small that we often feel stupid or petty even addressing them. "It must be my imagination," we think, "Why, we just had lunch yesterday and everything was fine." And yet, they act as though they have a problem. Well, they definitely do have a problem and their problem is *you*! They just are not going to be assertive and tell you about it. In fact, when you finally discover that all is not right with the passive-aggressive, and you confront them and ask, "Obviously you have a problem with me. What's wrong?," the number one response is, you guessed it, "Oh, nothing!" Not true! Trouble is definitely brewing, but they just do not want to let you in on it. Why? Because you might be assertive and work to rationally and maturely solve the problem, which is just what the passive-aggressive does not want. If you resolve the conflict, your suffering is over and that is no fun! The passive-aggressive does not desire an end to the difficult situation; they want it to go on indefinitely. Resolving issues is too easy. Their goal is to make you suffer, and they love to watch!

A passive-aggressive is the psychological equivalent of the Trojan horse: a friend to your face, a saboteur behind your back. Anything you tell them can and will be used against you—not today, perhaps, but sometime in the future when you are more vulnerable, which is why you must understand who they are. Secrets, confidences, and other issues you want no one else to know are dangerous in the hands of a passive-aggressive. I have seen situation after situation where an employee opened up their innermost private feelings to a coworker, only to discover to their horror that the confidential information was used against them at a later date.

WHAT IS AN EXAMPLE OF PASSIVE-AGGRESSIVE BEHAVIOR IN THE WORKPLACE?

Two of the most common examples of passive-aggressive behaviors that occur in the workplace are gossip and tattling. Surely you have experienced both of these either as a participant or a recipient, not only in business, but in other organizations and associations. Perhaps one person does not like another person, or they are jealous of someone. What a great way to stir the pot, create a little tension, and cause the other person a bit of grief—talk about them behind their back or tattle on them to their boss.

Here is a typical scenario: Jennifer and Sara work together and their desks are next to one another. They both take incoming calls from customers who have a question or complaint about their company's product. Jennifer is experiencing some personal problems with her husband and has been spending a considerable amount of time on the phone with him during working hours. This has gone on for several days. As a result, Sara has had to pick up more than her normal share of customer complaints and is not able to handle the load. Sara is understandably upset with Jennifer. Sara now has a choice. She can communicate her feelings in one of four ways. (Remember, we always have the following four choices.)

1. *Assertive.* Sara can talk to Jennifer face-to-face and explain that she understands and is sympathetic to her personal situation, but making personal calls on work time is not fair to Sara or the company. She can then share with Jennifer the amount of extra work she is having to pick up and ask that Jennifer make her calls on break or during lunch so the work can be done fairly and equally. If they are friends, Sara also may want to suggest other ways she might be able to help Jennifer through this situation and offer her support.

2. *Passive.* Sara can just grin and bear it. She can be a martyr and continue to work through her break and lunch, even stay after work, to handle the extra calls. On the outside, she appears fine—no problem. Although on the inside she is feeling both angry and frustrated. Because she is overworked, Sara has not been as patient with the customers as usual and several have complained to her boss who now wants to see her in his office. Sara's husband is also upset because she has been working long hours and comes home tired. In her attempt to avoid confrontation, she has ended up making everyone angry.

3. *Aggressive.* (a) Anger—Sara can get angry and let Jennifer know in no uncertain terms that she is being inconsiderate. "In fact," Sara yells, "no wonder you and your husband are having problems, if this is how selfish you are!" (intimidation). (b) Hurt—Sara can get her feelings hurt and take the entire situation personally. Instead of

blaming Jennifer's inconsideration on marital problems, she can internalize the problems and tell Jennifer, "You're always taking advantage of me. I've tried to be such a good friend to you and this how you treat me in return" (guilt).

4. *Passive-Aggressive.* Sara is angry but she is not about to let Jennifer know. She is going to make her suffer. In fact, when Jennifer apologizes about making personal calls and causing Sara more work, Sara simply shakes her head and says, "no problem." "Are you sure?" asks Jennifer. "Of course, I can handle it," says Sara. "I know you're having a tough time." Passive-Aggressives usually act as though everything is fine to your face, but then deviously plan to get even with what they perceive to be an injustice. Now Sara begins talking about Jennifer behind her back, telling other coworkers how angry she is and how inconsiderate Jennifer is. Sara also drops some fairly confidential information she has overheard when Jennifer has been on the phone. Other employees, who have always liked Jennifer, may adjust their opinion and begin to "side" with Sara.

Passive-Aggressives love to draw people to their "side" as though life were a battle and it's us against them. This serves two purposes. One, Sara likes knowing that others are mad at Jennifer, too. Two, Sara (and other passive-aggressives) need constant validation that they are right and the other person is wrong.

Sara could also resort to tattling. She asks to speak to her boss. Tattling usually goes like the following:

"Mrs. Williams, do you have a few moments? Now you know me. I'm not a gossip. [*Of course, she is a gossip or she would not have started her conversation denying it*]. It's about Jennifer. Now, I don't want to get her in trouble, [*Of course, she wants to get her in trouble—otherwise she would not be talking to Jennifer's boss behind her back*] but I think you should know that everyone is having problems with Jennifer [*passive-aggressives love to tag on other names to add credibility, instead of just admitting they have the problem. They use words like* we, everyone *or* all of us *instead of* I]. She is always on the phone with her husband during working hours, which is creating more work for me. [*Notice, the tattler often does have a valid complaint.*] Now, I don't mind helping her, [*obviously, she does* mind *helping her or she would not be tattling*] but we [*there is that* we *again instead of* I] are all having a tough time dealing with the situation. And please, whatever you do, do not tell Jennifer I talked to you" [*great—she has passed the problem onto the boss, and even demands confidentiality*].

See how passive-aggressives work? Now, we are not saying Jennifer is right. She should *not* be using work time to solve family problems, and she should *not* expect Sara to cover for her. But there are better ways for Sara to solve this problem and passive-aggressive behavior is not the answer.

Following are some other examples of passive-aggressive behavior in the workplace.

1. Bob has a great marketing idea. He shares it with a few colleagues at lunch. John immediately finds fault with the idea and, in fact, convinces Bob that it would never work. A few days later, John proposes the same idea to senior management and takes full credit.

2. Sandra is very jealous of Brad at work. He is fairly new to the job, but his customers love him. He has definitely caught the boss' eye. One day when Brad is at lunch, Sandra answers his phone and takes a message from a client asking that Brad call an important customer as soon as possible. Sandra conveniently "loses" the message causing the client and the customer to be angry with Brad when the call was not returned.

3. The purchasing department is overworked. They have been understaffed for a month and all have had to make a special effort to get products and supplies to the other employees in a timely manner. One day the purchasing manager informs them that the Sales Department has written a complaint letter about them directly to the CEO. The next time an important box comes in for the Sales Department, it somehow gets "misplaced" and is delivered even later than usual.

We could give hundreds of more cases. In each of the cases, someone is being taught a lesson by the passive-aggressive; however, because the other person is not even aware there is a problem, the lesson will be lost and nothing will change. Coming in late, leaving early, taking long breaks, and starting office rumors are becoming commonplace in a world where disgruntled employees seek revenge and retribution.

Do you notice a trend with passive-aggressive behavior? It is as though they are saying, "Fine! You want to take me on—then watch this. I'll make you sorry you ever messed with me!" Passive-Aggressives are at war, but it is a war of subterfuge and sabotage. Never underestimate the passive-aggressive—they can be simply annoying, but they can also be outright destructive.

Passive-Aggressive behavior at work can be especially devastating in a time when many people are concerned about the stability of their jobs. In the midst of mergers, reengineering, downsizing, and layoffs, it is scary to think there are people ready to take aim behind our back just when we need all the support we can get.

WHAT ARE SOME EXAMPLES OF PASSIVE-AGGRESSIVE BEHAVIOR IN OUR PERSONAL LIVES?

First, let's talk about marriage. Of the four communication styles, passive-aggressive is probably the most destructive in a marriage, next to abuse and addiction. A healthy marriage must be built on trust. Passive-Aggressive behavior is not about openness and trust; it is about secrecy and deceit. It is about getting even and making someone pay for perceived or real injustices. Passive-Aggressive tendencies split relationships apart leaving behind feelings of betrayal, hurt, and a desire to seek revenge in return.

Most marriages can endure and overcome a little passive-aggressiveness every now and then, but when passive-aggressive becomes the style of choice, the marriage begins to falter. Think about it for a moment. Healthy marriages begin with a commitment to help and support one another—not look for reasons to cause pain and anguish. When you walk down the aisle, hopefully, you see a person who you will be able to count on and one who can count of you. When these selfless feelings become selfish feelings, passive-aggressive behavior usually follows. Now, instead of thinking about what you can do for the other person, you are thinking about what they have not done for you and how you are going to pay them back for their inattention.

Most couples have a little score board in their minds, and they know what the score is in their marriage. Are they winning or losing? Do they control the other person, or are they being controlled? Or, is

the score tied with equal partners who support one another? Let's take a look at a typical scenario in a marriage.

John and Mary have been married for 10 years. They wake up one morning and both are feeling good about one another. The score is tied and neither partner feels taken advantage of or controlled; however, suddenly John decides he is going to play golf for a few hours. Mary is upset because she has got the house to clean, groceries to buy, the kids to take care of, and now John simply announces that he is out of the picture for the day. How does Mary handle this situation when she feels the score is now John—1, Mary—0? She is on the losing end.

Mary has the four choices we always have when we communicate our needs.

1. *She can be assertive.* Using *I* statements, she can tell John how she feels without resorting to threats, hurt feelings, or guilt. It might

sound like "John, I know you've worked hard all week and so have I. I also know that, like me, you'd probably like some time to yourself. How about we work something out that's fair to both of us. If you play golf this morning, I'll take the kids to their lessons and clean the house. Then, we can meet at the club for lunch. After lunch, I'll go on to do a little shopping on my own, and you could stop by the grocery store with the kids on the way home. I already have a babysitter tonight so you and I can both look forward to a little time alone together. Would this idea work for you?" Does this sound mature and sensible? Of course it does. Does it also sound like a fantasy? Unfortunately, the answer to that is often yes. What this conversation represents to most people is a magical trip through the twilight zone, because so many couples are used to communicating most often in one of the other three styles.

2. *She can be aggressive (using the attack word,* you). (a) Anger—"Fine, John, go ahead. You never think about me or the kids. You think you're the only one who works? What about me? All you do is work, watch football, and play golf. You don't pay enough attention to me or the kids. What am I supposed to do while you're off having fun? Clean and shop for groceries, I suppose" (intimidation). (b) Hurt—"Okay, go ahead and play golf [pouting]. No, I'm fine— really. One of us should have a good day; it might as well be you. No, children, it's all right. Yes, Daddy's going away *again*, but that's okay. Mommy will do something fun with you. Bye, honey—have fun [with a little tear]" (guilt). By using the aggressive style, Mary is hoping, through her anger or her tears, to make John feel bad about his choice to go golfing and decide instead to stay home in order to get rid of those bad feelings.

3. *Or, Mary could be nice, even though she is angry inside, and choose to be passive.* "Well, John, golfing sounds great. You deserve it. Don't worry about me. I'll make sure everything is done before you get home [martyr]. No, really, I'm fine, have a good time." If Mary really means what she just said, she was being assertive. *But,* she was being passive if she said these words and inside was thinking, "I can't believe he's going out today. He's got to know how much I need his help. I am so tired. When he's tired, I always notice and offer to help. I would never leave him alone with the kids if he'd had

the kind of week I've had. If he loved me, there's no way he'd play golf today. I need time alone, too." In fact, if this is how she really feels, then her nice response to John was an out and out lie. She is not fine at all and she does not think his idea to golf is great. Mary has totally misled John because she has not shared her true feelings. Can you see how the Passive style operates? Mary is being a martyr, hoping that John will read her mind and offer to help rather than being grown-up and assertive and stating her needs. Mary needs time, too, but she does not want to argue or make any waves so she just goes along and pretends to be fine. John goes off golfing, feeling comfortable with his day's plans.

4. *Mary could also choose to be passive-aggressive.* She will act as if nothing were wrong, but inside, she decides to teach John a little lesson in case he dares think about playing golf in the future and leaving her home alone. When John returns, he says, "Hi," and can immediately tell there is a problem. Mary says, "Hi" back, but her actions and tone let him know something is wrong. I did say earlier that in many cases it is impossible to tell for sure when someone is passive-aggressive, but they cannot resist dropping little hints, so they put on just enough of a show for you to be concerned or worried. If Mary acted completely fine, John would go about his business and that would ruin the passive-aggressive's plan for revenge. In this case, causing John to worry about what he possibly has done to make Mary angry is part of the pay-back process.

When someone is obviously upset, the natural question for us to ask them is, "What's wrong?" Passive-Aggressives love this question. They wait to hear this question because it means they did not drop subtle clues in vain. The object of their revenge took the bait. Now they can give the passive-aggressive's pat answer, "Oh, nothing's wrong." The stage is set. John cannot figure out what is going on, and Mary has no intention of telling him. Why? Because if she told him why she was upset, he might understand and offer to watch the kids so he could return the favor. Sounds like a good idea, right? Well, to the assertive, it would be the perfect answer. A grown-up solution. The assertive would take the offer and head out for an afternoon of freedom. But, a solution is not what the passive-aggressive wants, as strange as that may seem. They do not want to fix the problem, they just want revenge.

John, figuring Mary must not want to talk about something that probably had nothing to do with him (or so he assumes) begins to fix lunch. Every time he tries to initiate a conversation with Mary, she gives him a curt, one or two word reply, indicating she has no desire to talk. Finally, John tries to approach her again, saying, "Mary, something is obviously wrong. Are you mad? Did I do something?" Mary thinks to herself, "Of course you did something, but if you loved me, I wouldn't have to tell you." And her plan for revenge continues. She replies with anger, "I said I'm not mad. Can't you just leave me alone." John figures, "Well, something must have happened, but I guess it's not about me or she would tell me."

Now for the real pay-back—the silent treatment. She will probably not speak to John for several hours, which is about the amount of time he played golf. Remember, passive-aggressive is about evening the score, and in Mary's mind she was on the losing side. He played golf for 4 hours so she will give him a hard time for approximately the same duration.

John spends the afternoon confused, not knowing what is going on and Mary, in her mind, is in total control. By dinner, Mary has mellowed. The score is even again, so she starts talking. The problem is that now it is John's turn to even the score. In his mind, he has spent hours dealing with a silent, obviously angry wife who has not treated him very well and would not even tell him what her problem was and he has had it. It is time for John to teach Mary a lesson about what is going to happen if she acts this way again. Now it is John's turn to be sullen and unresponsive and Mary will be the one trying to get along. The games begin and the cycle of passive-aggressive behavior goes on and on.

The main reasons why passive-aggressive behavior is so destructive to a marriage are the following:

1. There is no honest communication. One partner (or both) is not telling the truth about how they really feel.

2. There is no attempt to find a solution or compromise because that is not part of the revenge process, so the problem cannot be resolved.

3. It becomes harder and harder to break the cycle because each person feels they have been wronged by the other and each is waiting for the other to apologize first.

Sometimes couples have been communicating passive-aggressively for years. Each one is waiting for the other one to say or do something nice first. Both are so busy paying one another back for real or perceived hurts that neither one is initiating any assertive or loving communication. If you were to question each of them, they would both claim to be the injured party and each would feel totally justified for any passive-aggressive behavior.

A successful, healthy marriage is based on mutual respect and trust that together form the basis for that feeling we call love. Passive-Aggressive is not about respect or trust. It is about revenge and retribution. It is difficult for a marriage to survive under these conditions.

I HAVE USED THE SILENT TREATMENT IN SOME OF MY RELATIONSHIPS AND NEVER THOUGHT OF IT AS A PASSIVE-AGGRESSIVE BEHAVIOR. WHY DO WE THINK NOT SPEAKING TO SOMEONE WILL HELP RESOLVE A PROBLEM?

Most of us pay people back by doing to them exactly what we would hate them doing to us, which is why women tend to use the silent treatment as a form of punishment more than men. Many women cannot stand it when someone refuses to speak to them. It worries them. They are afraid they have hurt someone's feelings or made someone angry and, therefore, are responsible for the silence. Some women will do almost anything to get the other person to speak to them again because of how insecure or uncomfortable they feel when someone manipulates by not speaking. The problem is that men do not usually view the silent treatment as a form of punishment. In fact, they usually view it as a reward! I had plenty of men tell me in therapy that they would purposely pick a fight on Sunday morning so their wife would get mad and stop talking! Why? You guessed it—so they could watch the football game in peace and quiet all afternoon while she was off sulking. Sometimes our attempts to get revenge backfire on us.

Passive-Aggressive behavior in a marriage is usually about control and who is going to give in first. If both partners are fairly stubborn, passive-aggressive behavior can continue for a long time with each person perceiving themselves as the innocent victim waiting in vain for the other one to apologize and give in.

Passive-Aggressives are rarely sorry for their behavior. In fact, the passive-aggressive usually feels totally justified using revenge tactics. They believe they have been mistreated and have a right to get even. You can see how these feelings can escalate in a marriage to a point where neither partner has any intention or desire to be loving, affectionate, compassionate, or cooperative until the score has been evened in their eyes. When two people reach this point, the marriage is usually difficult to salvage. It is very hard to feel love for someone while you are constantly thinking of ways to hurt, punish, or pay them back, especially if they are thinking the same things about you. This is why assertive communication is so important in a marriage. There must be a commitment to share feelings and concerns openly and honestly so passive-aggressive behavior can be avoided.

WHEN MY SPOUSE IS ANGRY WITH ME, HE (OR SHE) REFUSES TO BE AFFECTIONATE OR MAKE LOVE. ARE THEY BEING PASSIVE-AGGRESSIVE?

If one partner is angry or upset with the other, refusing to be affectionate may be the payback they choose. There are, however, certainly many physical, even emotional reasons why someone cannot or chooses not to engage in a physical relationship. Just because someone says, "I'm tired" or "I have a headache," does not mean that they are plotting a revengeful scheme behind your back. They may honestly be tired or truly have a headache. And if one partner is truly angry or upset, it may be understandable and reasonable for them to not want to be affectionate or physically intimate while experiencing those feelings.

If, however, a partner consistently withdraws affection every time they do not get their way or whenever there is a minor problem, or if there seems to be little or no indication that the other person has any interest in an intimate sexual relationship at all, then it would be only natural, even necessary, to look for the real cause.

As we said before, there is a major difference between sex and intimacy. One can have sex with a stranger and never even know their name, but trust, openness, and respect are required in order for two people to be intimate. When a partner is waging a passive-aggressive war against the other, trust and intimacy become almost nonexistent. Therefore, it is not usually an environment where intimacy is comfortable, enjoyable, desirable, or even possible, especially if sex or affection is being used to punish, control, or manipulate one of the partners.

Even though the refusal to be intimate and affectionate can be passive-aggressive, it is generally a valuable clue to both partners that there is a deeper problem that must be resolved. People stop communicating in the bedroom because they are not communicating well in all the other rooms of the house. When you are busy thinking of how to get even, it is hard to think of ways to be loving and romantic. When you are busy getting paid back, it is also hard to feel loving and affectionate. Physical intimacy is all about trust, which is missing in the presence of revenge, retribution, and other passive-aggressive ploys.

SOMETIMES I FEEL LIKE MY SPOUSE "SETS ME UP" JUST SO SHE (OR HE) CAN JUSTIFY GETTING ANGRY AT ME LATER. COULD I BE RIGHT?

Yes. Sometimes people set up a situation so they can justify being passive-aggressive by casting themselves in the role of the victim. For example, Tony never remembers birthdays. Ann has known for 10 years that Tony has never remembered her birthday. She could be assertive and tell him, "By the way, Saturday is my birthday. I'd love to have dinner out someplace romantic. I'll even make the reservations." Wow! Tell someone what you need and you may just get it. Ann could be sitting in an expensive restaurant having a great time, or she could set Tony up by not mentioning the upcoming birthday at all. That way, she can test him and see whether he really loves her. Unfortunately, Ann is also setting herself up because Tony probably will not remember, and she will spend her birthday crying and playing the victim nobody loves instead of celebrating. This is a definite set-up. Ann was looking for a reason to play the unloved wife and she knew exactly how to find it.

Another example is Jeremy. He has told Angela over and over again that she must get the oil in the car changed regularly. But with her busy schedule, full-time job and two kids, she often forgets. Jeremy knows from looking at the mileage that the car is due for oil again. But he does not say a word. Instead, he waits to see what will happen, even though he knows she will most likely fail the test he has set up for her. Then he can use it as even more "proof" that his wife is disorganized and inefficient.

Set-ups occur often in relationships. One partner has an unfavor-able image of the other and creates situations (*traps*, I like to call them) that reaffirm their negative perceptions. It is not difficult to see how a marriage might falter when partners are purposefully being set up to fail or look bad. The sad thing is, *both* partners end up being hurt by this passive-aggressive behavior.

CAN YOU GIVE SOME EXAMPLES OF PASSIVE-AGGRESSIVE BEHAVIOR IN CHILDREN?

Unfortunately, children seem to intuitively know at an early age what will work if they want to teach their parents a thing or two. With adolescents and teenagers, one of the most common passive-aggressive techniques involves their academic performance and grades.

Naturally, most parents have a sincere desire to see their children do well in school. Expectations for academic achievement are usu-ally shared with the children by the parents, and consequences are set and enforced if these expectations are not met. This is a healthy structure because children need boundaries, as we discussed earlier. In some homes, however, grades have become the major focus of conversation, which often leads to arguments and power struggles between the parent and the child. Although it is true that parents should set high expectations for school behavior and performance, the moment the child becomes aware that the grades are more im-portant to the parent than they are to the student, the child has been handed a loaded machine gun. They can now take aim and wound the parent anytime they want by simply bringing home a "D" or "F" and watching the adult's reaction.

I am not saying all low grades are a conscious attempt on the child's part to frustrate or anger the parents; but unfortunately, this is exactly what some students have in mind. Passive-Aggressive, like aggressive, is all about control and power. It is just done more subtly. If an adolescent or teenager feels out of control—too many rules, too many demands, too much criticism, and/or not enough freedom to participate in making their own decisions—then what a great way to regain a feeling of power: They can bring home bad grades and watch who is in charge now! The bottom line is that we cannot *make* a child do well in school and they know it. We can lock them in a room, tie them in a chair, spread out all the books and materials, tape their eyes open and their mouth closed, take away the phone, forbid them to see their friends, even ground them for life . . . but we cannot make them turn in the work or do well on a test without their cooperation. "But why?" you may ask, "would a child purposefully make bad grades just to get even with their parents? They are the ones who would get in trouble both at school and home!" Remember, people who use passive-aggressive behavior are often so intent on revenge and payback that they do not even realize they are hurting themselves far worse than their intended victim.

In the passive-aggressive's attempt to hurt others, they always end up hurting themselves as well.

The child is so intent on proving to their parents that they will not be controlled that they fail to visualize a future full of summer school and make-up work. Do not underestimate young people's knowledge of how the whole guilt process works. Sometimes we must help a child realize that these are their grades, not ours. It is their life, not ours, that will be affected by the choices they make now. Parents need to get out of the power struggle, and instead develop a partnership where they can assist their child's academic progress rather than order and dictate.

I can remember working with several young teenagers in a group counseling session. One student would be complaining about how strict his parents were when he brought home a "C." Before I could open my mouth, the other kids immediately explained how to turn the tables, "Bring home an 'F' or two, and next semester they will be paying you cash money for a 'C'."

Here is another classic scenario that is becoming increasingly more commonplace. Picture a divorced mother with a school-aged son—we will call him Bobby. In the absence of a father, mother and son spend a lot of quality time together and naturally grow close. Everything is fine until Mom remarries. Bobby is not thrilled about his stepfather, whom he views as an intruder. Nonetheless, with some strategic assistance from Mom and the new stepfather, Bobby could learn to adjust to the new family structure. Distracted and upset by all the sudden changes at home, Bobby's grades take a tumble for a few weeks. For the first time in his life, he brings home a "D" on his report card. He knows Mom is going to be angry, and he is worried about her reaction. Walking home from school, his mind works overtime on how he is going to explain it. The fact that he is thinking up excuses demonstrates that he recognizes his responsibility for his grades. So far, this has been a pretty functional home. Even though Mom has been alone, she has worked hard to provide a safe, supportive home with fair rules and boundaries. Bobby realizes he has not put the effort necessary into his schoolwork, and he is ready to tell his mom how he intends to bring the grade up next quarter.

Bracing for his mom's anger and disappointment, Bobby hands over the report card. Lo and behold, Mom does have an emotional outburst, but not the one he anticipated. Obviously upset, she says the most incredible thing, "I know I'm to blame for this!" Bobby's subconscious jumps into action. "Bobby, wait a minute," a little voice in his brain cries, "Don't apologize and tell her it's your fault. She thinks it's her fault. Play this out a little longer. If she's foolish enough to accept blame for your mistakes, then don't argue with her." So, Bobby plays along and mom continues, "I know how hard this has been for you. I haven't been paying enough attention to you, have I?" Bobby's "D" was for "distracted," not "dumb." He has caught on to his mom's guilt and is now ready to go on the attack rather than be on the defensive. "Yes, it is," he cries, "You care more about your job and your new marriage than you do about me! If you'd been here after school helping me instead of always at work, this wouldn't have happened." Notice how quickly someone can move into aggressive manipulation—sometimes all they need is an invitation from an insecure person. Bobby may not know the words guilt or manipulate, but he instinctively understands that what he earned with that "D" is control over mom.

When the new husband arrives home, he is met at the door by an anxious, guilty Mom, who shows him the report card. "I feel terrible about this," she cries. Stepdad will have none of it. A more objective observer, he believes that Bobby is responsible for his own grades regardless of the extenuating circumstances of his life. Calmly and reasonably, Stepdad explains this to Mom. "How can you be so callous?" she accuses. "His whole world has fallen apart. You don't understand. We used to do his homework together every day, and now I've been more involved with my job and you." He responds, "Callous? How can you be so irrational? My kids went through a divorce, too, and they didn't react by bringing home bad grades like your son."

The fight quickly escalates, much to Bobby's delight. He sees a wall forming between his mother and the man he sees as an intruder. Finally, she blurts out that from now on Stepdad will have no say in how Bobby is raised: "His father and I will go to school and deal with this! You just stay out of it!" Of course, it does not take an expert to know that such a fight provides nourishment to Bobby's more treasured fantasy: the reunion of his mother and father, with Stepdad out of the picture altogether. This scenario is so much better than Bobby ever imagined. His mom and her new husband are fighting. His mom is taking the blame for his lack of effort, and Mom and Dad will have to spend time together and all for the price of one "D" on a report card. Now tell me, with this kind of psychological reward, does Bobby have any incentive to improve his grades? Of course not. Why work at all when doing nothing pays such great dividends?

Sometimes children choose the silent treatment as a form of payback. As one teenager said to me, "Every time I try to talk to my parents about anything, they interrupt and start lecturing me or make me feel my idea was stupid. So, I just stopped talking. Now they say I'm too quiet, and they want to know what's wrong with me." Many parents of teenagers would complain to me that their children do not speak to them. Or if they do, it's that famous one word, *whatever* accompanied by a look and a shrug. I think these children used to talk to their parents, but got so tired of lectures, complaints, nagging, and criticism that they simply learned to avoid any discussion at all. I always suggest to parents that if they want to make one significant change in their family routine that could help a child be more secure, mature, and open, it would be this: Have dinner as a family as often as possible. Usually parents begin immediately to tell me how busy they are, the kids are, and on and on. I explain that that is the first problem: kids are too busy. They should not have every waking hour organized and scheduled—art on Mondays, soccer on Tuesdays, piano on Wednesdays, and so forth. My goodness, no wonder we have some kids on tranquilizers at 11 and 12 years of age—they never have time to be stress-free and relaxed.

Then parents tell me that even when they have dinner, the children (especially adolescents and teenagers) rarely talk. I think that is true only because we talk *to* them, *at* them, and *for* them most of the time. I have surveyed over 1,000 students, kindergarten through seniors in high school, asking many questions about the relationship between them and their parents. When it comes to the dinner hour, the majority described it as "an interrogation from the moment we sit down until the moment we leave." Perhaps in our busy lives, we want to fill every available minute at dinner with our captive children with "did you do . . .?," "how come your didn't . . . ?," "sit up straight," "you better not forget to . . . ," "what kind of look is that?" and so on. No wonder our children stop talking to us.

My advice to parents is to have dinner as a family *and* listen and share. Make a commitment that for at least 20 precious moments a day, they can be in a noncritical, nonjudgmental environment where they are not being lectured to or reprimanded. Because if a child receives mostly negative feedback, the likelihood is great that they will figure out how to regain control and get even, leading to a relationship full of passive-aggressive behavior.

Although children can and do use passive-aggressive behaviors when dealing with their parents, there are also times when what might appear to be passive-aggressive is anything but. Examples are hairstyles, clothing, and music. Many parents believe that their children purposely choose ridiculous hairstyles, strange clothes, or weird music just to make them angry. Usually, that is not the case. Peers, not parents, generally dictate those choices. However, if these choices reflect an inappropriate group of friends, then the parents would be wise to take notice and try to determine what they can do to help their child make better decisions.

DO PASSIVE-AGGRESSIVES GET THEIR NEEDS MET?

No. The irony of passive-aggressive is this: In their blind passion to get even, not only do they fail to get their needs met, they usually end up hurting themselves in their quest for revenge. Plus, the reason behind their revenge—the issue that made them spiteful and vindictive—is never even dealt with and thus, never resolved. That is why this communication style is such a sad waste of time and energy. Children who fail their classes in order to show their parents they are in control end up spending their summers going to school rather than being with their friends. The spouse who withholds love and affection to teach a lesson misses out on being held and touched. The coworker who gossips, trying to create a clique of supporters, loses the trust of everyone who hears the gossip.

Passive-Aggressives choose to sacrifice their relationships, gaining at best the hollow satisfaction of watching others become confused and frustrated for a short while. At times everyone feels powerless, but we must fight the urge to get even, for it is not our place in the cosmic scheme of things to teach others their lessons. It is enough to learn our own lesson, which is simple: to assert ourselves, deal with issues head-on, and try to resolve and mediate our conflicts as professionally and maturely as possible. When we do those things, we can short-circuit any rationale for behaving passive-aggressively. There is no gain in revenge—"An eye for an eye," as Gandhi said, "leaves the whole world blind." Resist the temptation to feel yourself wrongly treated, instead ask for what you want and then be willing to assertively work toward healthy, respectful relationships.

Summary

- Passive-Aggressive behavior can destroy a relationship.
- Passive-Aggressives act one way to your face and another behind your back.
- It is often difficult to identify a passive-aggressive person because they are sneaky and devious.
- Passive-Aggressive is about paying someone back for a real or perceived injustice.
- Passive-Aggressives justify their revenge tactics because they believe they have been victimized and have the right to get even.
- Giving someone the silent treatment is a technique of the passive-aggressive.
- Passive-Aggressives usually end up hurting themselves in their pursuit for revenge.
- Gossip and tattling are common forms of passive-aggressive behavior.

Take Action

- Identify a relationship where you have used passive-aggressive behavior. What did you do in your attempt to get even or pay them back? Did it work?
- The next time you feel like getting even with someone, try being assertive and letting the other person know how you feel in an honest, forthright manner.

9

DEALING WITH THE PASSIVE-AGGRESSIVE PERSON

In any situation where you suspect passive-aggressive behavior, you must begin by taking a close look at yourself and your communication style. This is not to excuse the passive-aggressive in any way, because their behavior is definitely unhealthy, nonproductive, and sometimes even hurtful. However, as we have learned repeatedly throughout this book, (a) we play an integral part in how people treat us and (b) we can change ourselves, but we cannot change others. So, we first need to evaluate our own behavior so we can determine if we are possibly contributing to an environment that allows passive-aggressiveness to grow and thrive.

In order for someone to be motivated to seek revenge, they must first identify what appears to be, in their mind, an injustice done to them. Paybacks are about evening the score. So, in the case of our relationship with them, they are reacting to us and to what they believe we have done to them. That does not mean we necessarily really did anything that was wrong, but we must recognize that *they* perceive and believe our behavior to be inappropriate, unacceptable, unfair, or unjust. Unfortunately, there are times when they are right—our behavior was one or all of those things. Their covert, devious reaction is still not excused, but we have a place to start when trying to diffuse the passive-aggressive.

IS THERE A COMMUNICATION STYLE THAT IS MOST LIKELY TO SET OFF PASSIVE-AGGRESSIVES?

Without a doubt the aggressive angers the passive-aggressive the most; therefore, we need to look at our own communication style and determine whether we have a tendency to employ aggressive manipulation involving hurt or anger in our relationships. When most people are faced with aggressive behavior, it is usually difficult for them to respond assertively. As we have discussed, communicating assertively requires several things, including (a) an understanding of how assertive should sound based on past experiences with assertive role models, (b) the confidence in oneself to treat others fairly and be treated fairly and respectfully in return, and (c) a commitment to maintain healthy and functional relationships.

Responding assertively to the constant barrage of aggressive manipulation and intimidation takes great skill, courage, self-esteem, and even a sense of humor. Unfortunately, many people respond to the aggressive by either becoming equally manipulative (yelling back, threatening, crying, etc.), or avoiding the confrontation and being passive. We have learned that neither of these work—at least not in the long run. If we become aggressive, we lose because the aggressive loves it when they can get us to yell or cry. When we stay passive, we lose because they will only come on stronger next time because they are led to believe we cannot set limits.

So now what? It appears we have tried it all and the aggressive is still in control. As days, weeks, and months pass, we become more and more frustrated. There must be some way, we say to ourselves, to get even. Thus, the beginning of passive-aggressive thoughts creep into our subconscious.

WHAT KIND OF PERSON USES PASSIVE-AGGRESSIVE BEHAVIOR?

Most likely, we have all used passive-aggressive behavior in our relationships at one time or another, but the predominantly passive person is likely to use passive-aggressive techniques most often. The assertive avoids sabotage at all costs and, therefore, resists passive-aggressiveness. The aggressive does not even try to be sneaky. They are so sure of their ability to control others that they want people to know just how angry or hurt they really are. It is the passive, the oh-so-nice, whatever-you-want-is-fine-with-me person who often resorts to getting even behind your back. Passive-Aggressives are often people who believe their lives are controlled by others; but they lack the skill, knowledge, desire, and/or confidence necessary to be assertive, and they sense that outright aggression will get them into trouble. Their answer: manipulate (aggressive) but do it so no one knows (passive). Do not underestimate the passive. They appear to give in and go along, but their passive-aggressive personality may be working overtime to tip the scales back in their favor.

DOES THIS APPLY TO ALL PASSIVE PEOPLE?

For the most part, yes. It is not normal or healthy for anyone to be controlled for long periods of time by another person in a relationship. As a species, we are blessed with the ability to reason and the opportunity to make choices based on that reasoning. We are not programmed to just go along passively, but rather to be independent and thoughtful. When we find ourselves in a manipulated and controlled environment where we are not allowed (or feel we are not allowed) to be an integral part of the relationship, we usually begin to experience some inner conflict. Those voices inside of us start whispering, "You have a right to speak up," "This isn't fair," "What about your feelings?" and so on. Again, we have those same four choices.

1. We can continue to be passive and remain in a manipulative, controlled environment.
2. We can learn to be more assertive so we can deal with our environment in a functional, healthy way.
3. We can let it go until we finally "lose it" and become aggressive, choosing to match manipulation for manipulation.
4. We can go underground and get even while appearing on the surface to continue to go along. This is passive-aggressive.

DOES THE PASSIVE USE PASSIVE-AGGRESSIVENESS ON PURPOSE?

Yes and no. Unfortunately, so much of what we do and say is done without thinking: we just react. So, some passive-aggressiveness may occur without premeditation, but simply as a reaction to behavior we do not like or do not appreciate. For many people, passive-aggressive behavior is a way of life and many good people are passive-aggressive at some time in their lives. Silent treatment, gossiping, and setting people up are passive-aggressive behaviors that many people use on a daily basis. Passive-Aggressive behavior never fixes the problem and often makes it worse. As we have said before, we are always responsible for our actions; therefore, we *must* make a conscious decision to *not* simply react or behave in a way that just "feels good" for the moment, but rather weigh the choices so both our actions and our communication serve to enhance our relationships rather than destroy them.

On the other hand, most passive-aggressive behavior is done on purpose; in fact, considerable time has been spent thinking about what can be done to get even. Passive-Aggressives live their life with a score board and know no other way. They want to teach you a lesson without you knowing what they are doing, and they often delight in their pursuit to exact their revenge.

DOES THE PASSIVE-AGGRESSIVE
ENJOY MAKING OTHERS SUFFER?

Unfortunately, yes. It is an unhealthy enjoyment, almost sick, but passive-aggressive is a very sick, unhealthy behavior. Remember, passive-aggressive is about evening the score and paying someone back. Having their victim suffer, in their eyes, is the surest way to even the score. That is sick enough, but the fact that they are willing to hurt themselves in the process is really dysfunctional and indicative of their unhealthy frame of mind. Their revenge never gets them what they want. In fact, it moves them further and further away from their goals. Passive-Aggressives make things worse—not just for their victim, but for themselves.

BECAUSE PASSIVE-AGGRESSIVES ARE
SO UNDERHANDED AND SNEAKY, WHAT CAN
WE DO TO MINIMIZE THEIR ATTACKS ON US?

Be as assertive as possible. That is not to say assertive people do not also have some passive-aggressives in their life. There will always be people who need to blame something or someone for their own problems, but the assertives often can keep the passive-aggressives in their life at a distance or at least minimize their destructive tendencies. Why? Because most passive-aggressives find it no fun to deal with someone who will openly and honestly call them out about their behavior. Most assertives have no time for passive-aggressive behavior. For example: If a passive-aggressive gives the assertive the silent treatment, or pouts, watch out! The assertive may grow tired of the childish passive-aggressive behavior, assertively question their behavior, then go about their business. There is nothing more frustrating to the passive-aggressive than to have their behavior addressed assertively. They want to pout, roll their eyes, yawn, or give you the silent treatment for hours without being accountable. Most passive-aggressives have never had to be accountable for their behavior and, therefore, are led to believe that they can continue their underhanded sneaky ways without being held responsible.

HOW DO PASSIVE-AGGRESSIVES REACT TO THE AGGRESSIVES IN THEIR LIVES?

Many people began using passive-aggressive behavior when they had a close relationship with someone aggressive. Aggressiveness not only attracts passive-aggressiveness, but often is responsible for passive-aggressive thoughts to begin to glimmer in someone's mind. When you are trying to control someone aggressively, the odds are good that at some point they will turn on you. If you are lucky, they will shower your attempts to manipulate with a dose of assertiveness; but this does not happen often. Usually, they will avoid hurting you or making you angry and will give in to your demands (passive). You think you have won, but as time goes on, the chances are good they will plot and plan a way to get revenge and you will never know what hit you.

DOES PASSIVE-AGGRESSIVENESS EXPLAIN SOME OF THE VIOLENCE AND TERRORISM IN THE WORLD TODAY?

Without a doubt. The world is full of people exacting their revenge on unjust (real or perceived) acts done yesterday, last year, and maybe even 100 years ago. Sometimes, passive-aggressive behavior is totally and unequivocally unwarranted. Nothing was done to provoke it. For example, a person may be angry, not because of anything done to them, but just because of what someone represents (i.e., a policeman, a teacher, a politician, part of the "establishment," a different race, gender, sexual orientation, etc.). In these cases, the passive-aggressive is not out to get anyone personally, but they are angry at a situation or a system, and others just happen to be in the wrong place at the wrong time.

When you look at some of the sad, seemingly meaningless threats, bombings, and violence in the world today, you can see how passive-aggressives can literally destroy not only a relationship, but a culture or a nation. We can look at some of the groups who are fighting over what appears to be insane reasons and wonder, "Why don't they just work this out peacefully before thousands more are killed?" That would, of course, be the assertive reaction. But to the passive-aggressive, it is not about mediation, negotiation, or even peace—it is about pain, suffering, and retribution. It is about someone who feels totally justified participating in any and every action (even murder) in their attempt to even the score or teach someone a lesson.

We have witnessed some of these organizations working desperately to negotiate a settlement, only to watch as others refuse to be a part of any agreement to exist peacefully and choose, instead, to continue the horror. Why? Because passive-aggressive is not sane; it is not rational, it is not fair, and it is not ethical. It is always hurtful with the intention of inflicting pain—emotional, mental, or even physical. Passive-Aggressives have no desire to make peace—with a spouse or a nation—until the appropriate payback (according to them) has been doled out. Sadly, there are some people who seem to be so caught up in the payback process that they lose all desire to ever be at peace. These people are scary and dangerous. It is very difficult to deal with this type of passive-aggressive.

GIVE AN EXAMPLE OF HOW WE CAN MINIMIZE PASSIVE-AGGRESSIVE BEHAVIOR AT WORK.

Vicki and I are often asked to speak on the topic of team building. We include in that presentation an entire segment on gossip and tattling, because these passive-aggressive behaviors can literally destroy a department or team. Most of us went through a phase in our early childhood when we tattled, but we should have outgrown that behavior. Unfortunately, many people have carried that childhood phase right into their adult workplace. The problem is many leaders today contribute to a work culture where management not only allows gossip and tattling, but accepts the responsibility of following up on the tattler's gripes and complaints, or even contributes to the gossip themselves.

When we work with leadership and teams, we begin by telling them:

1. Tattling should not exist in a functional, healthy workplace.
2. It is not your responsibility to listen to the tattler.
3. It is not your responsibility to fix the tattler's problems.
4. It *is* your responsibility to teach the tattler assertive communication techniques that they can use to resolve their own problems face-to-face with other people.

There are only two reasons any employee should "tell" on another employee. One is if the other person is doing something illegal. The other is if the other person is doing something unethical. These two situations are not considered tattling. Tattling is all the other petty little complaints people have about one another. Tattlers learned at an early age how to be passive-aggressive: if you do not like someone, tell on them and get them in trouble—that will teach them a lesson!

Let's see how we can change this dysfunctional tattling environment to a more assertive climate. First, employees should always know that if anything is illegal or unethical, they can discuss it confidentially with their boss or management. Otherwise, the scenario should go like the following:

Sara: "Mrs. Barnes, do you have a moment?"

Manager: "Sure, Sara."

Sara: "It's about Jennifer, she . . . ."

Manager: "Wait a minute, Sara. Did Jennifer do anything illegal or unethical?" (Remind the employee of the two reasons why they should be telling on another employee.)

Sara: "Why, no, but . . . ."

Manager: "Then, let me ask you one important question. What did Jennifer say when you discussed this problem with her?"

(This reminds the employee that she *should* have discussed the problem with Sara first.)

Sara: "Well, I haven't really talked to her about this."

Manager: "Why not?"

Sara: "Well, that's your job."

Manager: "No, Sara, my job is to help you learn the necessary skills to talk to people face-to-face. So, think for a moment. What would happen if you talk to Jennifer personally? What's keeping you from sharing this with her?"

Now, the assertive manager moves into conflict resolution and problem solving. Leadership is not about doing everyone's work for them. It is about teaching others through your leadership how they can solve problems on their own. Managers who really want to stop gossip and tattling should say next, "Sara, stay here. I'm going to call Jennifer in my office so the two of you can work out a solution." Of course, Sara is aghast! But, as a manager, the messages given are the following:

1. Gossip and tattling are not allowed in the workplace.
2. I am here to help you learn to resolve your own conflicts respectfully.
3. If you have a problem with another employee, you need to be mature and first talk to them about it face-to-face.

Tattling can be stopped *if* management wants to stop their own participation in the process. Vicki and I always remind managers that it is impossible to have a team that can work effectively and cooperatively together if tattling is allowed. Teams need to trust one another and trust cannot exist in an environment where employees must worry about whether others are talking behind their backs and tattling about them to their boss.

Office gossip is another passive-aggressive behavior. Many employees say they are tired of the gossip, and yet they continue to contribute. "But I don't participate in the gossip," many say, "I just listen and keep quiet." Well, keeping quiet *is* participation as far as the gossip is concerned. They will take your silence as evidence that you agree with every word they are saying. Gossips do not care if you add to their gossip or just hang around and listen—it is all the same to them. So, you can either stop the gossip, walk away from the gossip, *or* you can stay and be a part of it. There are no outside observers in this arena.

HOW CAN I JUST WALK AWAY? I HAVE TO WORK (OR LIVE) WITH THESE PEOPLE.

You are right. It is not easy to walk away. It is hard for two reasons:

1. *Many people really enjoy a bit of gossip.* It is reassuring for them to talk about other people who they do not think are as cute, smart, talented, and so forth, as they are. Gossiping is, for many people, a way to feel better about themselves.

2. *Sometimes we are afraid to stop the gossip because they might turn on us next.* We would rather participate and have someone else be the victim than take a stand and become the victim. But, please note that the gossip is talking about all of us at some point anyway. No one is safe from their spiteful tongues. If, however, we take a stand and speak up for others who are being talked about, maybe someone will do the same for us. The gossip is not the person whose respect we should be trying to earn. Our own self-respect should be our concern.

DO GOSSIP AND TATTLING CREATE EVEN MORE PASSIVE-AGGRESSIVE REACTIONS?

Most certainly. Let's take a typical workplace scenario. The day shift is angry at the night shift for not organizing the office before they left work. Now the day shift could be assertive by coming in a little earlier than usual and assertively talking to the night shift people, "We know you all are busy just like we are. Sometimes, however, when we come in the next morning some of the paperwork is not in the right place and is hard for us to locate. How can we help you fix this problem? Is there anything we can do to have things more organized for you to give you more time, in return, to help us?"

Oh, how mature and grown-up. Also, how rarely that happens! Instead, here is what usually takes place. The day shift people complain

to their supervisor, who, instead of teaching them how to react face-to-face with the evening employees, takes on their problem and goes to the night shift supervisor. That supervisor calls a meeting and tells his staff, "The day shift is complaining about us again." Now, do you honestly think these people now say, "Oh, the poor day shift. We need to work harder so they can be happier." I doubt it. By being passive-aggressive, the day shift has assured that the night shift will follow suit and become passive-aggressive as well. In fact, the day shift should prepare themselves because the odds are good that things will be even more disorganized than ever. Please remember:

> *Passive-Aggressive behavior almost always produces a passive-aggressive reaction.*

The night shift says to themselves, "Oh, yeah. They don't like how we do our job. Well, they should try working all night sometime. Let's see how they like this!" The night shift becomes even more determined to let the day shift struggle just to teach them a lesson.

ISN'T IT BETTER SOMETIMES TO JUST IGNORE PASSIVE-AGGRESSIVE BEHAVIOR RATHER THAN DEAL WITH IT ASSERTIVELY?

Never! Remember, any behavior that we ignore will happen again. Because our avoidance and unwillingness to deal with the situation has given them the message that we will allow and accept their behavior, we become responsible for their behavior. Let's look at another example from work: Often, during employee-staff meetings, there are one or two employees who are visibly passive-aggressive. The boss is relating some new ideas to the entire department, and there are two staff members sitting with arms folded, rolling their eyes, heaving sighs, and making snide comments to the person next to them. "Well, that's not very sneaky," you say. "I thought passive-aggressives always did things behind your back." Not always. These employees are not being passive and keeping their feelings silently to themselves. And, they are not being aggressive and angrily attacking the boss or the idea. Instead, they have chosen to be passive-aggressive and make their objections known without really dealing with the issue.

In most cases, the manager ignores this behavior, because they are concerned if they take them on, there will be a scene. Well, we must learn to confront passive-aggressives or they, like the aggressive, will just get worse. But, do not take them on aggressively by getting into a power struggle. Do not use hurt or anger. Do not go on the attack and push them into a corner. This is not the place for a verbal battle between the boss and the obviously disgruntled employee. Also, do not get your feelings hurt and try to make them feel guilty for not agreeing with your plan. Instead, be assertive. "Helen, you seem to disagree with this plan. I could be wrong, but the way you've rolled your eyes, heaved a few long sighs, and made some comments would lead me to believe you have some concerns. Is that correct?" This is called *checking it out*. You just want them to publicly acknowledge their feelings about this issue. Most passive-aggressives, just like most aggressives, have never had to be accountable for their actions; therefore, they feel totally comfortable acting anyway they want.

Now, the passive-aggressive has two choices:

1. *They can lie and say, "Oh, I have no problem whatsoever with this plan."* That is great news for you. Now you can make them head of the committee, have them write a report, or do research on the

project. They will soon learn to avoid passive-aggressive behavior. They have no desire to be put to work—they just wanted to complain without being held accountable for their behavior.

2. *They can tell you the truth and say, "Well, as a matter of fact, I think this plan is going to fail for many reasons which are . . ."* Now, your true character comes out. How do you respond when someone disagrees with you or gives you negative feedback? Many people revert to aggressive and use either hurt or anger to stop the criticism in its track. The goal of hurt would be to make the employee feel guilty that they disagreed or criticized. The goal of anger would be to make the employee afraid to criticize or disagree. Most defensiveness is usually a combination of the two: a little hurt and a little anger.

When someone disagrees with us in a public forum, how we respond is very important. This is one of the hardest times to be assertive, but one of the most necessary times. The best assertive response to someone who disagrees with us is, "Thank you. I appreciate your willingness to tell me how you feel face-to-face." *Thank them,* you might say incredulously? You bet! We might as well hear what they are thinking about us to our face because they are saying it behind our back anyway. Remember, passive-aggressives are at war with us. Every great general knows that you will never win a war unless you have a really good idea what the enemy is thinking. That is the only way to predict and intercept their next move. The same strategy holds true for the passive-aggressive. Unless we know how they feel, we will never be able to plan a successful strategy to help improve the relationship. Good leaders are excited when their staff brings contradictory thoughts to the table so they can formulate their plans based on both the pros and the cons of any given situation.

IS PASSIVE-AGGRESSIVE BEHAVIOR ALWAYS DIRECTED AT US BECAUSE OF SOMETHING WE DID?

Unfortunately, no. That is why this is such a difficult behavior with which to deal. I remember speaking to a group of employees at an in-service training workshop. It was a mandatory meeting, and many of them were angry at the senior management team because they felt they had not been asked to participate in the decision to bring in an outside speaker. When I walked on stage and began to speak, three employees picked up a book at the same instant and began to read. I knew instantly that this was not being directed at me. I had barely even opened my mouth. This was a passive-aggressive gesture toward the administration. What they were saying indirectly was, "OK, you can make us come, but you can't make us listen!" (See how utterly childish passive-aggressive usually is?)

Should we ignore passive-aggressive behavior when it is not directed at us?

No way! I may not have been the source of their problem, but they brought their anger into my space. I assertively said, "For 17 years I taught students at all levels, elementary through high school, ages 6 through 18. I was a good teacher and a fair teacher, but never in 17 years was a student allowed to behave rudely in my class. When someone spoke in our room, we each listened with respect. Today you need to know, I would accept no less from a 40 or 50 year old in terms of mature, respectful behavior than I would from a 7 or 12 year old. You can participate respectfully or you may leave." Two stayed and put their books down and ended up loving the session. One of the employees left, which was fine with me. Remember, assertive people set fair boundaries. The one thing that did bother me, however, was later when a manager said to me, "Good for you! It's about time someone took them on. They're always reading, talking, and not paying attention during my staff meetings!" Hmmm . . . I wonder why? They had a leader without the courage to set limits. No wonder they felt they could bring their passive-aggressive behavior into another meeting.

Tardiness is another passive-aggressive behavior. Often when someone does not want to meet someone, go to a meeting, or is angry at the person they are meeting, a great way to get even is to be late. Vicki and I are very assertive when it comes to starting meetings on time. Often our meeting planners will ask, "Do you mind if we start 10 or 15 minutes late so we can make sure everyone is here?" Our answer is always, "Yes, we do mind. We will be talking about how people should not reward negative behavior; therefore, it is important that we model that message. The people here on time make a concerted effort to do the right thing. They should not be punished and asked to sit idly waiting on a few who *choose* to come late." It is amazing how fast the word gets around. Now, we go to the conferences where audiences have heard our philosophy and you know what? They figure out a way to be there on time! Vicki and I tell our leadership sessions that the average meeting starts 12 minutes late!

Do you know how much wasted time per month that is? When that occurs, even punctual people learn to be late. Remember:

We train difficult people.

HOW CAN WE DEAL WITH PASSIVE-AGGRESSIVE BEHAVIOR IN A MARRIAGE?

Oh, you know the answer! Be assertive! Remember John and Mary earlier in the book who both got caught up in paying each other back? Each one hurt because their spouse did not pay attention to them. Well, someone has to break the cycle in a passive-aggressive relationship and that is not always easy. We have said over and over again that assertiveness takes courage and self-esteem.

Here is another example: A wife who wants her husband to pay more attention to her moves into passive-aggressive. She gives him the silent treatment and withdraws affection. Not only does he not get closer and give her more attention, he withdraws even more than before and stays longer and longer at the office.

Which partner is going to stop the cycle of paybacks and spiteful acts and begin doing loving things again? We talked about a scorecard—who is winning and who is losing? At first glance, it would seem that to stop the cycle and be the first to make the move to be more loving would really be losing. But, both people are losing now. They are losing trust, respect, tender touches, and laughter. Most important, they are losing their relationship.

There is *never* a winner with passive-aggressive behavior, only losers.

The true winner is the one who can stop acting like a child and begin acting like a healthy adult. The true winner is the one who can begin to communicate assertively and lead the way toward a more fulfilling and loving life. There are no losers in a happy, healthy relationship.

When we talk about being the first one to give in, we are not referring to abusive, addictive relationships. Giving in and apologizing to hurtful, addictive, or abusive people is going to keep the dysfunctional cycle going on and on. But in a nonaddictive, nonabusive relationship between two people who have just gotten off track and carried away with some nonproductive behaviors, it is the winner who intervenes. It is very sad that when we need love and attention the most, we often become the angry, bitter, and nagging kind of person who is the hardest to love.

If we want to be loved, we must be loving.

SO HOW DO WE BREAK THE PASSIVE-AGGRESSIVE CYCLE IN OUR PERSONAL RELATIONSHIPS?

Stop keeping score and begin being a loving person again. Do nice things without keeping track of whether the gestures are returned. Smile more. Be more affectionate. When we are being passive-aggressive, there is very little physical intimacy. Who wants to hug, kiss, or make love with someone with whom we are angry? Give yourself a month to just be loving, generous, and kind without worrying or watching to see if every little gesture is returned.

Be the kind of person you would like others to be to you.

Then, see what happens. You will probably experience some nice moments for a change. It is amazing how quickly the people in your life will respond to your thoughtfulness, your tenderness, your generosity, and your openness. Doesn't being assertive feel good? Also, avoid aggressive behavior. Do not use either hurt or anger to get your spouse's attention. It will only push them further into passive-aggressive.

HOW CAN WE DEAL WITH SOMEONE WHO GIVES US THE SILENT TREATMENT IN A NONWORK SITUATION?

You guessed it—assertively! Manipulation using the silent treatment within a marriage is probably one of the oldest and least effective strategies used by partners who have a definite problem with their spouse or significant other. As we discussed before, women use this strategy more often even though men are the least affected by it and usually view it as a reward (at least until the football game is over). Women seem to be the most affected when someone refuses to speak to them. In fact, many women will apologize, even when they do not know what they did, just to stop the war of silence.

First, tell them you are totally aware of their attempts to get even with you for some perceived injustice (and it may be a very real injustice) by saying, "OK, it is apparent that you aren't speaking to me and this seems somewhat foolish for two reasons. If you are upset or angry with me, there is no way for me to understand what I did unless you tell me. Also, if I don't know why you are angry, we can't work on fixing the problem. Refusing to speak to me does nothing to help us figure this out, but I realize I cannot make you talk. Therefore, I'm going to go about my business until you are ready to discuss the situation with me."

Then, do just that—go about your business and just let them sulk until they decide to deal with the problem in a more mature, assertive way. Do not let their silent treatment work on you! Teach them that you will be fine while they are not speaking and are perfectly willing to wait until they decide to grow up and communicate assertively.

BUT I THOUGHT WE WERE NOT SUPPOSED TO IGNORE NEGATIVE BEHAVIOR, BECAUSE THAT WOULD CAUSE IT TO CONTINUE.

Well, that is true except in the case of the silent treatment for two reasons.

1. We should never ignore behavior that is inappropriate, unacceptable, unethical, or illegal. The silent treatment is none of these. The person is just being childish by sulking and refusing to speak.

2. Ignoring their silent treatment is exactly what they cannot stand. They are dying for you to give a reaction—any reaction will do. To not react drives them crazy and is the one thing that will ensure they finally break down and begin to speak again.

Please refrain from matching their passive-aggressive behavior by refusing to speak to them. Giving the silent treatment back just results in those icy, terrible periods where neither person speaks for days or weeks. That is simply double manipulation. Plus, returning the silent treatment is resorting to using passive-aggressive yourself, so in a way, they have won. Do just what we suggest—go about your business and act as though nothing is wrong. Picture a situation where a mother has put a child into time-out and the child is standing with their arms folded with a downcast, mean look. What does Mom do? She goes about her business doing the housework, fixing dinner, taking a bath, reading a book, and so forth. Pretty soon it becomes tiresome to keep the mean looks and downcast demeanor.

The same technique works on children, friends, and coworkers. The silent treatment is only effective when the other person cannot stand the silence and chooses to give in and react.

WHAT CAN WE DO WITH CHILDREN WHO USE PASSIVE-AGGRESSIVE BEHAVIOR?

One of the examples we previously gave of passive-aggressive behavior in children involved grades. As teachers, both Vicki and I can give every parent some advice. Do not take the full responsibility of your child's grades away from them. As we said before, if your child figures out that their grades are more important to you than to them, you have handed them a loaded machine gun that they will point at you every time they want to get even and be in control.

As a parent, your responsibility is:

1. To provide a clean, quiet, safe environment for your children to do their homework.
2. To provide a time to do their homework that is radio, telephone, and television free.
3. To provide the materials and resources needed to do their homework.
4. To offer to help and support their needs. This can be in the form of rides to the library, computers and software for research, tutors, and making yourself available to answer difficult questions.

A parent's job is *not* to sit at the table with their children night after night going over every question and checking every answer.

There are many parents today who literally do their child's homework for them. If you do not believe us, try looking at some of the science projects at the school fairs. You will be astounded at the amazing things 5 year olds can do!

Sometimes in our attempts to rescue kids from any negative consequences we fail to teach them an important skill they will need in order to be successful as adults: responsibility.

ARE YOU SAYING THAT I SHOULD ALLOW MY CHILD TO FAIL?

Once in a while, yes. Children need to know that there are consequences. If failing or working below their potential becomes a habit, then of course we would do everything possible to help them sort out the reasons why they are not successful. Once in a while, however, it is good for a child to learn that when one does not follow the rules, does not manage their time, does not listen to instructions, or fails to do the assignment, there is generally a price to pay. Homework grades are an indicator to the teacher of how well a child or an entire class has learned a lesson. Sometimes parents, by doing the child's homework, fail to provide the teacher an important barometer that suggests whether their students understood the material. If a parent notices that their child cannot do the homework on their own on a regular basis, then they need to make an appointment with the teacher and discuss the problem.

WHAT IS THE BEST WAY TO APPROACH MY CHILD'S TEACHER WITH A PROBLEM?

Sometimes parents resort to using passive-aggressive behavior when they deal with their children's teachers. Rather than assertively making an appointment with the teacher to discuss the options, they instead help the child at home without ever letting the teacher know there is a problem, whereas at the same time they gossip to other parents about what a bad teacher their child has. Meanwhile, they also call the superintendent and school board members to tattle on the teacher behind his or her back. Now we know there are teachers who may not be doing as good a job as the parent would like; however, assertively making every effort to work with the teacher face-to-face models the best approach to the child who learns by watching the parents. If that does not work, then the parents can assertively move to the next step of meeting with the principal and teacher to resolve the problem.

HOW DO WE HANDLE THE SUBJECT OF GRADES SO OUR CHILDREN WILL NOT USE THEM AS A LEVER FOR CONTROL?

Usually it is not about the grades themselves. The issue is about control. We realize this is a difficult area because in order to be good parents, we must have a certain level of control. Even in our definition of a functional, healthy home, we said that it is imperative that fair, consistent rules and boundaries be set and enforced. But, here is where some families diverge from assertive and set the stage for a passive-aggressive child who is looking for a way to get even.

1. *Are the rules fair?* If not, passive-aggressive behavior will invariably exist. Children know they have little or no say about their life and how they are treated. There are so many rules and so many expectations. Children also seem to intuitively know that loving parents should be setting limits so, for the most part, they accept the rules with little rebellion if the rules are fair! But, if the expectations and rules are way out of line, too rigid, unnecessary, or punitive, they will fight back as best they can. And often that rebellion is in the form of passive-aggressive behavior. How can they get even with a situation that is not fair? They will use silent treatment, bad attitudes, breaking curfews, "forgetting" to do chores, or bringing home bad grades, to give just a few examples.

2. *Are the rules consistent?* Maybe the rules and expectations are fair but they do not apply equally to every child. Children know which rules apply to which sibling. If they perceive themselves as the victim, the child upon whom tougher rules are placed, chances are they will move into passive-aggressive to even the score.

IT SOUNDS AS THOUGH IT IS VERY IMPORTANT TO CLEARLY TELL OUR CHILDREN WHAT WE EXPECT OF THEM.

Most definitely. The more a child understands what is expected of them and taught why those rules and expectations are relevant to their future well-being, the less likely they are to engage in passive-aggressive behavior. Remember, children will model the behavior of their caregivers. If a child consistently sees his or her parents trying to even the score with passive-aggressive tactics such as pouting, withholding love, silent treatment, gossiping, or tattling, the child will soon begin to use those tactics as well. Not only must we share our expectations, but we must also let our children know what the consequences will be if those expectations are not met. The more involved the child is in these discussions, the more they will understand about accountability and responsibility for one's actions.

SO ASSERTIVENESS IS THE KEY TO DEALING WITH PASSIVE-AGGRESSIVE JUST AS IT WAS WITH THE OTHER COMMUNICATION STYLES?

Yes—pretty easy, isn't it? We only have one style to think about, learn about, practice, and integrate. Be prepared, however, because the passive-aggressive will surely test your assertive limits. If you can deal with them and their manipulations, your life will be much easier.

Summary

- Passive-aggressive behavior almost always produces a passive-aggressive reaction.
- We train difficult people.
- There is never a winner with passive-aggressive behavior, only losers.
- Do not ignore passive-aggressive behavior or it will get worse.
- Passive-aggressives are not used to being held accountable for their behavior.
- The only time it is beneficial to ignore negative behavior is when you are dealing with someone who is giving you the silent treatment.
- Just as with other communication styles, assertive is the only way to effectively deal with the passive-aggressive.

Take Action

- Is there someone in your life that deserves to be taught a lesson? Are you tempted to get even by using passive-aggressive behavior? If so, how could you communicate your feelings more assertively?

- Watch for passive-aggressive behavior in your relationships at work and home. Notice how destructive it is. Think about ways you could improve communication.

- Do you have someone in your life who is being passive-aggressive to you? Do you know why? Think about how you could begin to communicate more assertively and productively with them. Have you let them know you are aware of their behavior?

EPILOGUE

You now are familiar with the four communication styles. These four styles represent the choices we have every time we relate to and communicate with other people in our lives.

I NEVER KNEW COMMUNICATION WAS SO COMPLICATED.

That is the problem. Most people do not think about communication at all. They usually listen (sometimes only half-listen), then react without thinking, saying the first thing that comes to mind. If they do take the time to plan what they are going to say, it is usually because they are planning something sneaky, mean, or manipulative. Unfortunately, we tend to spend a long time planning what to say when we are being critical, hostile, defensive, angry, or judgmental. It is very sad how many people have interpreted what is one of our most important constitutional rights—the Freedom of Speech—as permission to manipulate, exaggerate, hurt, misrepresent, intimidate, and invade the privacy of others. Surely that is not what our forefathers had in mind.

Just remember, communication really does not have to be so complicated. Assertive communication is the only healthy choice, so focus your attention on becoming a person who uses that as your one and only communication style.

188

WHAT DO WE DO NOW THAT WE HAVE ALL THIS INFORMATION ABOUT COMMUNICATING?

As always, you have choices. You can simply do nothing, write this book off as an interesting read and continue to communicate and be communicated with in the same way as always. Unfortunately, statistics show that is what about 70% to 80% of you will do. Why? Because making a decision to change ourselves, our attitudes, and our behavior is hard work. Also, blaming others for our problems and waiting for them to change seems so much easier. But, it really is not easier.

It is not easy to wait for others to change.
It is much easier to change ourselves.

This book is about taking control, not of others, but of yourself. It is about taking control of your life and your relationships, your job, and your future. Most important, this book is about taking control of your assertive ability to make choices and to then take responsibility for those choices.

THIS BOOK WAS NEVER REALLY ABOUT THOSE "OTHER PEOPLE," WAS IT? THIS BOOK WAS ALWAYS ABOUT ME.

Yes, it was. If you truly understand that, then maybe you will be part of the 20% who will read this book, take action, and begin to change your communication style, your attitudes, and how you react to other people! We hope so, because you and you alone are the only one who can change your life for the better.

INDEX